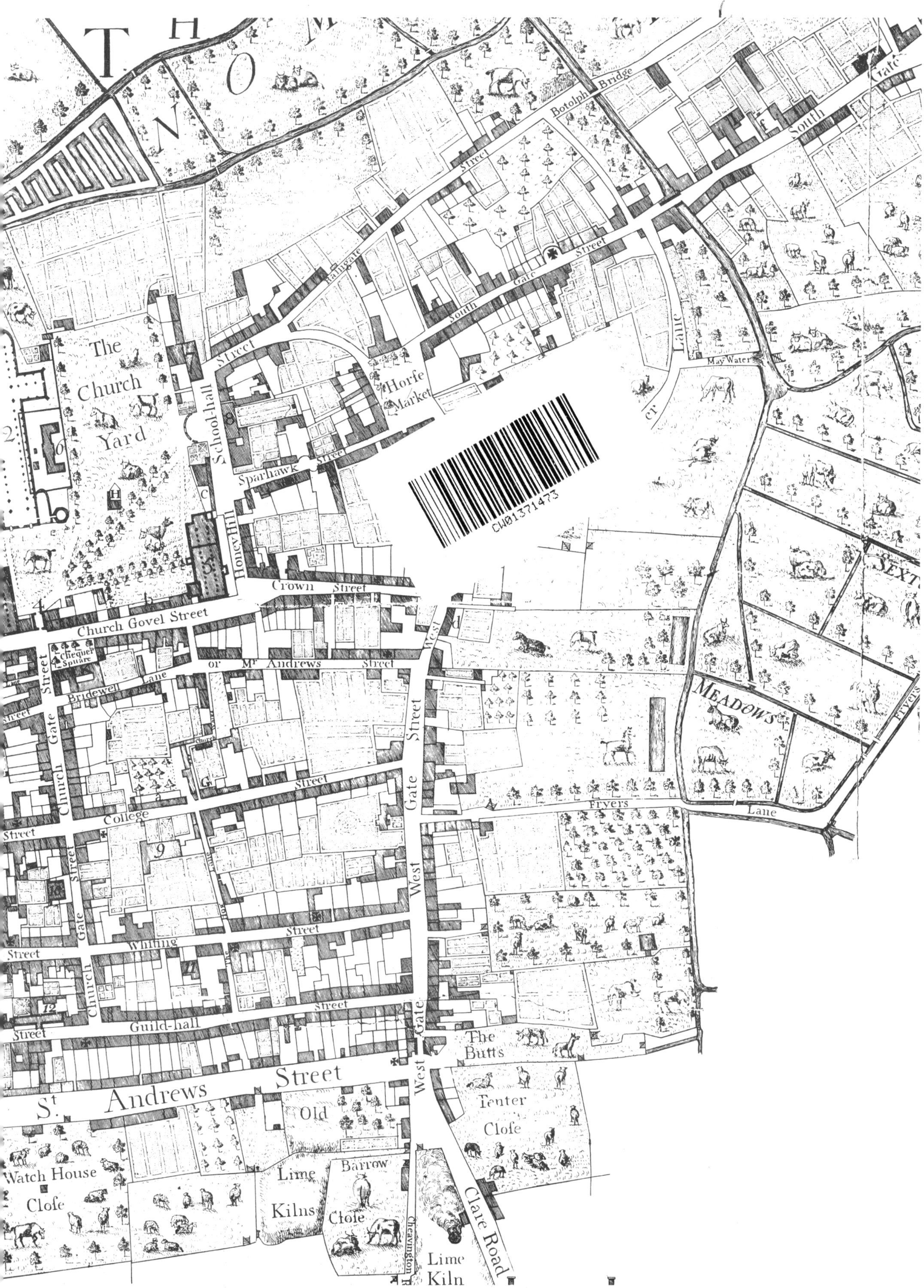

T. H O M
O
N
Botolph Bridge
South Gate
Street
Street
Ramgate
South Gate Street
Lane
May Water
The Church Yard
School-hall Street
Horse Market
Sparhawk Street
Honey Hill
Crown Street
Church Govel Street
Chequer Square
or Mr Andrews Street
Bridewell Lane
Church Gate Street
West Gate Street
Street
College Street
MEADOWS
SEXT
Fryers Lane
Fryers
Whiting Street
Guild-hall Street
St. Andrews Street
The Butts
Old
Tenter Close
Watch House Close
Lime Kilns
Barrow Close
Chevington
Lime Kiln
Clare Road

THE BOOK OF BURY ST EDMUNDS

FRONT COVER: J. C. Smith's 'The Norman Gateway', 1809. The ground level round the tower had built up level with the road; cupola, clock face and projecting dial have been omitted. The Queen's Head on the right and house on the corner of Athenaeum Lane had not then been faced with brick. (V&A)

The wolf guards St Edmund's Head, from a 12th century manuscript which contained the offices used on St Edmund's Day, 20 November. (M.736 f.16 The Pierpoint Morgan Library, New York)

THE BOOK OF BURY ST EDMUNDS

BY

MARGARET STATHAM

BARON BIRCH
MCMXCVI

ORIGINALLY PUBLISHED IN 1988
& IN THIS REVISED EDITION
BY BARON BIRCH FOR THE BARRACUDA COLLECTION
FROM QUOTES LIMITED IN 1996

PRODUCED BY KEY COMPOSITION, CHENEY & SONS
HILLMAN PRINTERS (FROME) & WBC BOOK MANUFACTURERS

© Margaret Statham 1988 & 1996

All rights reserved. No part of this publication may be reproduced, stored in a retrieval system, or transmitted, in any form or by any means, electronic, mechanical, photocopying, recording or otherwise, without the prior permission of Quotes Limited.

Any copy of this book issued by the Publisher as clothbound or as a paperback is sold subject to the condition that it shall not by way of trade or otherwise, be lent, re-sold, hired out or otherwise circulated without the Publisher's prior consent, in any form of binding or cover other than that in which it is published, and without a similar condition including this condition being imposed on a subsequent purchaser.

ISBN 0 86023 576 9

Contents

ACKNOWLEDGEMENTS	8
FOREWORD BY THE BISHOP OF ST EDMUNDSBURY & IPSWICH	9
INTRODUCTION	9
BEDRICESWORTH	10
RELICS OF RENOWN	25
THE WAYS OF THE LORD	43
ABBEY AND BOROUGH	54
THOSE IN NEED	65
RULES AND REGULATIONS	78
BURYE WORKE	89
FOR YOUR AMUSEMENT	102
LESSONS LEARNT	117
IN OUR OWN TIME	126
POSTSCRIPT, 1996	140
APPENDIX – POPULATION	141
BIBLIOGRAPHY	142
INDEX	143

Acknowledgements

In the thirty years I have lived in Bury St Edmunds, I have been fortunate in having the opportunity to meet and talk with many people who have been interested in the history of the town, some as searchers at the Record Office, some as members of the Past and Present Society and others quite informally. It would be impossible to thank them all by name, but I am grateful to every one of them. My greatest debt of all is reflected in the dedication of this book.

In writing this book, I am much indebted for the help I have received from Amanda Arrowsmith and her staff at the Suffolk Record Office and to Anne Partington-Omar and her staff at the Museum. Hilary Hammond at the Central Library introduced me to my publisher and I have always had a friendly welcome from all members of the library staff. I owe great debts to Norman Scarfe, David Dymond, Peter Northeast, Diarmaid MacCulloch and Stanley West.

The pictures are undoubtedly the best part of this book, and I am most grateful to all those who have allowed me to reproduce material from their collections. Without the co-operation of the Suffolk Record Office and the St Edmundsbury Museum Service it would have been very difficult, if not impossible, to gather together this number of prints, drawings and old photographs. Many friends have helped me in this and my debts are reflected in the credits to the pictures, but two must be mentioned specially; John Knight, who made available an album of prints, and Oswald Jarman, who put at my disposal his private collection of photographic prints of the town.

My daughter, Helen, has always encouraged me and I am pleased that one or two of her photographs have been used. My friend David Baynes-Cope has discussed all the text with me, and helped me in many practical ways. I am most grateful to them both.

Special thanks are due to the Bury St Edmunds Central Library, the Suffolk Record Office (Bury St Edmunds Branch), Moyses Hall Museum and the Clock Museum for keeping the essential subscription files, without which publication would not have been possible.

NOTE to the 1996 Edition: In the ten years since the first edition was researched, archaeological and documentary research has inevitably modified some detailed aspects of the town's past. Equally, there have been modern changes in townscape and commerce. These, together with minor errors of fact or production, have been amended where practical. Recent publications have been listed. A brief Postcript records principal events.

Key to Caption Credits

BFP	*Bury Free Press*	RF	The Very Revd Raymond Furnell
BJH	Mrs B.J. Hill	RH	R. Hill
HS	Helen Statham	RWE	Mollie Elliott, for photographs taken by the late R.W. Elliott
JA	John Agate		
JK	John Knight	SAU	Suffolk Archaeological Unit
OGJ	O.G. Jarman	SRO(B)	Suffolk Record Office, Bury St Edmunds Branch
JC	From a drawing by John Clibbon		
PM	Pierpont Morgan Library, New York	SRO(I)	Suffolk Record Office, Ipswich Branch
PPS	Prudential Property Services	St E	St Edmundsbury Museum Service
RCHM	The Royal Commission on the Historical Monuments of England	V&A	Victoria and Albert Museum

Foreword

by the Bishop of St Edmundsbury & Ipswich

Although I have been Bishop of St Edmundsbury & Ipswich for only a year, my knowledge of Bury St Edmunds stretches back over thirty. In no way, however, can it be compared with the deep and loving knowledge of the town which Margaret Statham so ably presents in this book. It gives a living and vibrant picture of the history of the town, covering many periods and not ignoring the present day. Those who are interested in learning and deepening their knowledge of the Cathedral town of Suffolk will find it fascinating for reference and reading. I shall be making steady use of it myself.

John St E bds ad Ipswich

Introduction

It has always seemed strange that a town which, for many years, invited passers-by to stay in historic Bury St Edmunds did not have a history. There are a number of studies of particular periods or themes, and there are editions of some of the many important series of documents relating to the town, but no one book which sketched the whole period of the town's history and covered a variety of topics.

Some years ago, in conversation with Norman Scarfe, we decided that Bury ought to have a three volume history. My experiences of the last few months have confirmed this view for, in a short book, it is impossible to discuss points which ought not to be stated baldly; and, of course, a book of this length means that much more has to be left out than is put in. The first two chapters I drafted ran to over 17,000 words in the original version.

I hope this little book will help people to understand how the town has come to be as it is and, above all, that it may encourage others to study some of the many aspects of the history of Bury St Edmunds which have not yet been studied.

Dedication

In Memory of
Martin Purefoy Statham
1921 — 1974

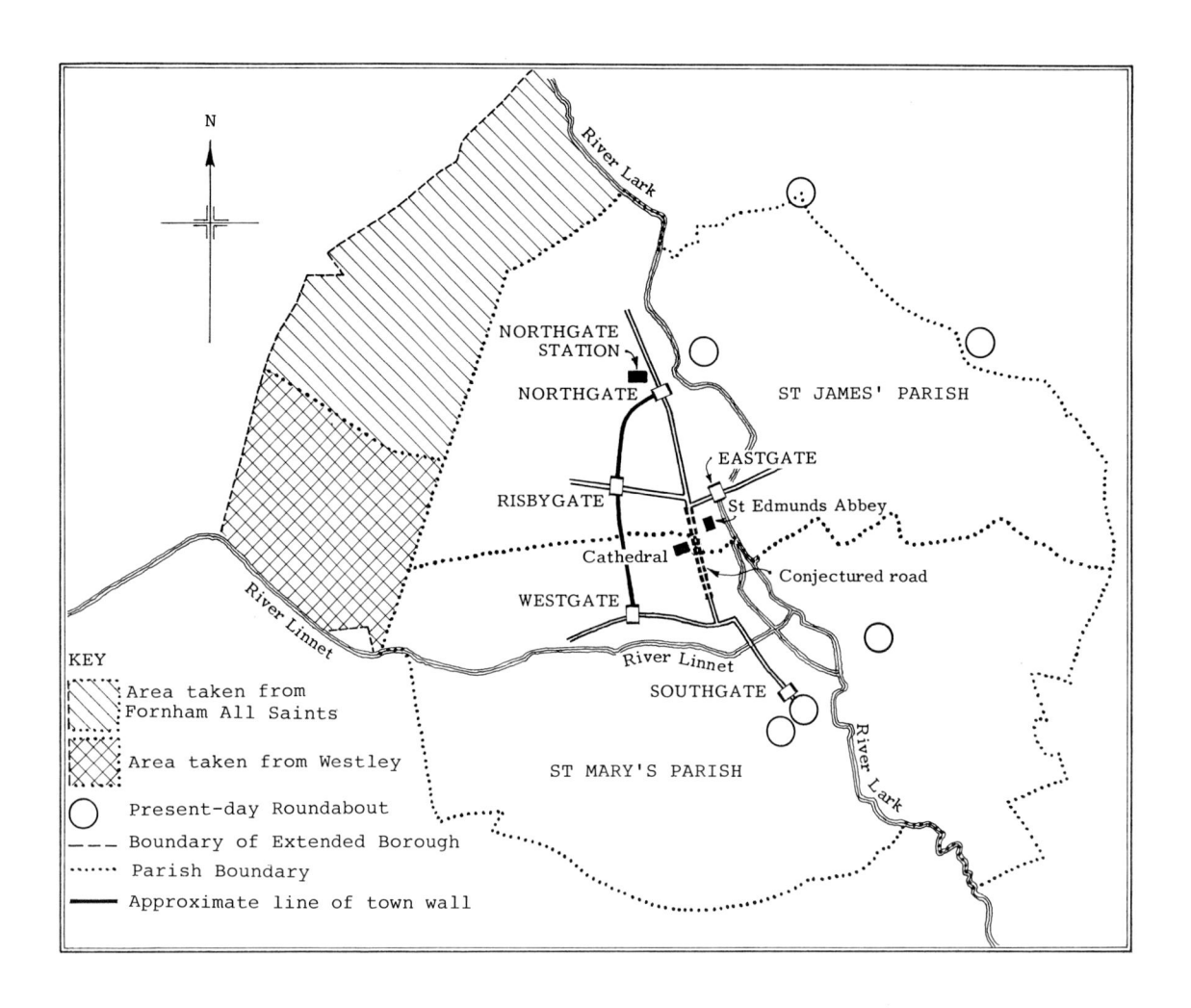

Plan showing ancient borough boundary, town gates, presumed line of town wall, parish boundaries, line of pre-conquest road connecting High Street (now Northgate Street) and Sparhawk Street, land taken in under the West Suffolk Review Order, 1934.

Bedricesworth

Bury St Edmunds is on the river Lark, which joins the Great Ouse near Ely. The name Lark is derived from Lackford, a village on the river between Bury St Edmunds and Mildenhall, and is of no antiquity, while its tributary was given the name Linnet because of its similarity to Lark. Until the eighteenth century, the Linnet joined the Lark by the Abbot's Bridge but the two now meet further east, at the end of the garden of the house in the Churchyard called Abbey Precincts.

The Lark valley attracted settlers from early times, and some of those people left archaeological evidence of their presence in what is now Bury St Edmunds. There is no known Roman precursor for the town, but three Anglo-Saxon cemeteries, indicating that there were nearby settlements, have been found in Westgarth Gardens and Barons Road, which are on the edge of the *banleuca*, and a third in Northumberland Avenue on land taken in from Fornham All Saints in 1934. Ipswich-ware pottery, which dates from c625-c850, has been found in the course of excavations on the site of the King's House, within the precinct of the Abbey itself. This shows that Bury St Edmunds was a 'new' foundation, which fits the view that Sigeberht, King of the East Angles, founded a monastery here c630. Apart from this reference, the town disappeared from the pages of history until some time after the death of Edmund, King of the East Angles, who was killed by the Danes in 869 and was, within a few years of his death, venerated as a saint. From an early date, valuable offerings were made to St Edmund among which one of the most notable was the gift by his namesake, King Edmund, in 945, of the land which surrounded the saint's shrine. This became a highly privileged area, known as the *banleuca* of St Edmund, within which the Abbot was to enjoy all but regal powers. This area was defined by four stone crosses and it is possibly the base of one of these which still survives, and now stands in the grounds of the West Suffolk College. It is now called the plague stone, because the hollow into which the shaft fitted is reputed to have been used to contain vinegar as a disinfectant for money, during an epidemic, but the stone probably formed the lower part of the Risbygate Cross, which originally stood somewhere in Out Risbygate, not far from St Peter's Hospital.

Some scholars have questioned the authenticity of King Edmund's grant of land in 945, but there can be no doubt that its boundary clause was written during the Anglo-Saxon period, nor that the boundaries of the land it defined were to be the boundaries of *Bedricesworth* and, later, Bury St Edmunds, until additional land was taken in from the surrounding parishes of Fornham All Saints and Westley, as a result of the West Suffolk Review Order of 1934.

As a Royal town or *villa regia*, *Bedricesworth* was likely to have been a place of more than ordinary size and importance from an early date. The pre-Conquest town lay parallel to the river and consisted of a north/south road, represented by Northgate and Southgate Streets today, which converged on the town's first market place, now called St Mary's Square, and there formed a junction with Westgate Street. This road, it is believed, originally ran across land which later became part of the Abbey precinct, and joined Northgate Street with Sparhawk Street. At the time of writing, there is a possibility that Dr S.E. West, the County's Principal Archaeological Officer, will soon be excavating a length of this road, which he identified just north of the Cathedral in 1983; the trial excavation revealed traces of buildings along the road, while late Saxon pottery was found in one of the road ditches.

Whenever the rest of the shire paid geld to the Crown, the inhabitants of Bury St Edmunds, as we can rightly call it by the time of William the Conqueror, paid a sum to the Abbey instead, so there was no reason to have an entry relating to the town in Domesday Book. The entry we have, unusual in form and content, is difficult to interpret in every detail, but nevertheless it is of outstanding interest and full of information which could not be obtained from any other source. Of especial importance in considering the physical development of the town is the statement that, in the twenty years between 1066 and 1086, no less than 342 houses had been built on land which had formerly been under the plough and, as it is also said that the town's value had doubled, it seems reasonable to assume that the town's size had doubled too. The driving force behind this rapid expansion was undoubtedly the French physician, Baldwin (formerly a monk of St Denis in Paris) who became Abbot in 1065. He was Edward the Confessor's physician before the Conquest, and held the same office under William. During his abbacy, not only did the building of the Abbey church and conventual buildings, of which the ruins can be seen today, begin, but he also appreciated the advantages to the Abbey of a thriving town at its gates, so he encouraged skilled craftsmen to settle, many of whom would have been employed about the monastic buildings.

Where Abbot Baldwin built their houses is not known. It is often asserted that he was responsible for the town plan as we know it today, with its enormous market place which, before it was eroded by later buildings, extended from Palmers on the east to the Royal Bank of Scotland on the west; Barclays Bank on the south to Moyses Hall on the north. However, Abbot Anselm (a nephew of St Anselm and formerly Abbot of St Saba at Rome), who took up the building of the Abbey church with great vigour between 1121 and 1148, enlarged Baldwin's original conception. The result was that both the ancient Parish Church of St Mary and the Parish Church of St Denis, built by Baldwin, had to be demolished and re-sited at the western edge of the precinct. Thus in Baldwin's time a large part of what is now the precinct may well have been available for other purposes, and it is possible that Baldwin's original settlement was sited near the Abbey church; as High Street was the first name for Northgate Street, it could be that the road crossing the precinct remained for a time the main street. There certainly seems to be no compelling reason why the area in which the churches were later built need either have been within the precinct, or empty before Anselm's time.

An important feature of the town plan is the so-called great axis, the line of Churchgate Street which leads directly to the main entrance to the churchyard, through the gate known in the past as St James Church Gate, the Cemetery Gate or just the Church Gate, and which we call the Norman Tower. A glance at the map will show that the principal entrance to the great court of the Abbey, which is now known as the Abbey Gate, is not quite in line with Abbeygate Street. This gateway was rebuilt after the riots of 1327, when the townsmen destroyed an earlier entrance gateway along with many other monastic buildings. Obviously it was intended that there should be a similar axis along the present Abbeygate Street to the entrance to the court, but, when the gate was rebuilt, it was necessary to build the new gateway beside the old one, which must have been repaired as soon as possible and kept in use until its handsome successor was finished. The precinct was probably extended during Anselm's abbacy, so perhaps this feature of our town plan should be attributed to the Italian Abbot Anselm, rather than to the French Abbot Baldwin.

The built up area of the town was enclosed with a stone wall and gates during the time of Abbot Anselm. Although there are literary references to the stone wall, no trace remains; an excavation in Tayfen Road indicated that there was only an earthen bank behind a ditch, but this may simply indicate that the lie of the land demanded no more. The five gates were pulled down by order of the Corporation between 1761 and 1765 but we know where they stood; there are still places along the line of the wall where the rise of the ground on which it stood can be seen, although these are much fewer than they were thirty years ago, as so many of the businesses in St Andrews Street and Guildhall Street have levelled the wall sites in their gardens for car parks. If the gates of the Bushell yard in St John's Street happen to be open, that is as good a place as any to observe this feature.

Some of the earliest surviving deeds of town properties confirm statements in *Gesta Sacristarum* (an account of the building work of the Sacrists) that Anselm caused walls to be built around both town and precinct, for these refer to properties in relation to the gates of the town and precinct. There is also documentary evidence for a ditch which surrounded some of the precinct; observation of surviving traces, revealed by trenching for repairs to public utilities, suggests that this was about 15 feet broad, and that it extended from St Mary's Church along Crown Street and Angel Hill, presumably flowing into the river by the East Gate. Bridges, which would have been necessary to allow access to the precinct, are mentioned in the account of the rioting which took place between Abbey and town in 1327, and are shown in early drawings.

Those houses described in the early deeds had their living accommodation *(solar)* on the first floor, while the shop or workshop *(domus)* was on the ground floor. It was usual for vendors to reserve the right to the use of these ground floor shops for themselves, to let to whomever they could during the time of Bury Fair which, as it was one of the most important trading fairs of mediaeval Europe, made space within the market extremely valuable.

Apart from the local flint, building stone had to be brought long distances at great expense; much of the stone for the Abbey church came from Barnack in Northamptonshire, while some came from as far away as Caen in Normandy. Secular buildings were usually timber-framed, but some were built of stone, and Moyses Hall remains an example of one of these early stone houses. Remains of Norman workmanship survive in a number of other houses, while there is literary evidence for some in deeds and in the *Chronicle of Jocelin of Brakelond*. The townsmen, for instance, built stone houses in the market place, to enable them to pay a regular rent to the Cellarer, in lieu of the reaping services they were once compelled to perform, while others were built by Abbot Samson as an endowment for the monastic school.

One stone house was near Paddock Pool, at the east end of Churchgate Street, close to the Norman Tower; a 1713 deed of the Athenaeum defines its site on the west as abutting on Punch Lane, otherwise Paddocks Pool, while much earlier references show that the properties on both of the northern corners of Bridewell Lane abutted on Paddock Pool to the north. Deeds from the time of Abbot Samson give a rare glimpse of the development of this part of the town, one building site there being no less than 90 feet long by 53 feet wide.

In April 1430 Abbot Curteys made an agreement with John Arnold and Herman Remond to burn bricks for him at Chevington and, a little later in 1463, John Baret suggested that brick might be suitable for rebuilding the Risbygate, for which he left a bequest. How soon brick came into regular use is difficult to say, but one has only to look around to realise that timber remained the usual building material for a long time. In the 18th and 19th centuries many timber-framed buildings were faced with brick, to give the town a deceptively Georgian appearance; there are many demure-looking 'Georgian' houses which are much older, as one can see as soon as one goes through the front door or looks at the back or sides of such buildings. On the whole, the Georgian townscape is only skin-deep.

Fire was an ever-present hazard in towns whose principal building materials were wood and thatch, and Bury St Edmunds experienced one of these harrowing occasions on 11 April 1608 when, 'through the sleepy negligence of a servant', fire broke out in a malt house in Eastgate Street which belonged to a maltster called James Randall. This, like most houses in Bury St

Edmunds then, was thatched. An account of the fire forms the preamble to a bye-law, designed to prevent the use of thatch as a roofing material on any new houses built, or for completely re-roofing old ones. This records that 160 dwelling houses and 400 outhouses and 'houses of necessary use' were destroyed, a total loss not less than £60,000. A picture of the damage caused by this fire is gradually emerging as more and more deeds reveal which properties were devastated. A stiff breeze carried sparks from one thatched roof to another along Eastgate Street and into at least part of Northgate Street, across the road up Looms Lane, and thence into the market place. The fire certainly reached as far as the corner of Woolhall Street on the west side of Cornhill, much of the Traverse, and many properties in the present Buttermarket, probably including the Suffolk Hotel. There is no sign of the fire having damaged property on the present Angel Hill or in Abbeygate Street. Probably, apart from Moyses Hall, there is nothing now above ground in the market place which ante-dates this fire, although there is older work in many cellars. Rotten Row, before the fire, ran from the north west corner of Cornhill south as far as the Market Cross; the Guildhall Feoffees bought the site and, apart from part of the north end of the Cross, it was never rebuilt — perhaps it already caused traffic problems in the early seventeenth century.

No new road or street was laid out in the town from mediaeval times until the 19th century when Prospect Row, off Kings Road, then known as Field Lane, was built. This short row of houses, which first appears on Lenny's map of 1823 as St Edmunds Place, was to herald a long period of steady expansion, typified by streets such as Victoria and Albert Street in the western part of the town. Orchard Street and others in the St Johns Street area reflect the increased importance of that part of the town, following the coming of the railway in 1846, when St Johns Street became the normal route for railway passengers making their way to the town centre.

Despite the considerable areas of agricultural land used for building, by the 1930s building land within the borough boundary was scarce, and the land taken in from Westley and Fornham All Saints under the West Suffolk Review Order of 1934 provided the space needed for extensive post-war development.

To what extent the Lark was viable as a means of transport in early times no-one knows; that the water table was once much higher is certain. There is much evidence of heavy goods shipped from London to Lynn, and thence brought to the town overland, and river carriage must have been used whenever possible for heavy goods such as stone. The Lark was, however, made navigable to Fornham St Martin in 1698, while late in the 19th century it became possible to bring coal by water to a point behind the Keymarket Store in Mildenhall Road.

The Gough map shows that Bury St Edmunds stood on the only main road which ran through Norfolk and Suffolk, that is the main road from London to Norwich, through Cambridge and Newmarket; later on, a network of roads connected the town with Sudbury, Thetford, Newmarket, Stowmarket and Ipswich. Road transport in early times was difficult and costly. The dualling of the A45 (now A14) in the early 1970s must be regarded as a major event.

By the beginning of the 17th century—and probably long before—the town carrier and letter carrier made regular journeys to the capital each week. In an order of the Corporation dated 20 July 1613, the town carrier was required to leave on Monday rather than Tuesday so that, for the better observation of the Sabbath, he might return on Saturday rather than Sunday; the letter carrier was also enjoined to arrange his journeys so that he need not travel on Sunday. By 1782, when details of the postal service can be found in a local guide book, the post left the general post office in Crown Street for London every morning, except Saturday, and returned every evening apart from Monday. The Norfolk post then left every evening except Monday and returned every morning except Saturday.

More and more regular coach services carried goods and passengers, mainly to London, but also to other places. An enormous improvement in communications came when the station in

Northgate Street and the Ipswich and Bury St Edmunds Railway were opened at the end of 1846. Amid scenes of great enthusiasm, a crowd of several thousand greeted the first train in to the town from Ipswich, after a journey lasting from 12.43 to about 2.30pm. The line was extended to Norwich *via* Stowmarket in 1849, and to Cambridge in 1854. In 1852, the Eastern Union, the East Suffolk, and the Eastern Counties Railways were amalgamated, to be known eventually as the Great Eastern Railway, which undertook to complete the lines connecting Long Melford, Clare, Haverhill and Lavenham with Sudbury, Bury and Cambridge, and subsequently connected Bury with Thetford. From 1865 to 1909 there was a second railway station in Eastgate Street, for trains on the Bury and Sudbury line. This was demolished before 1924.

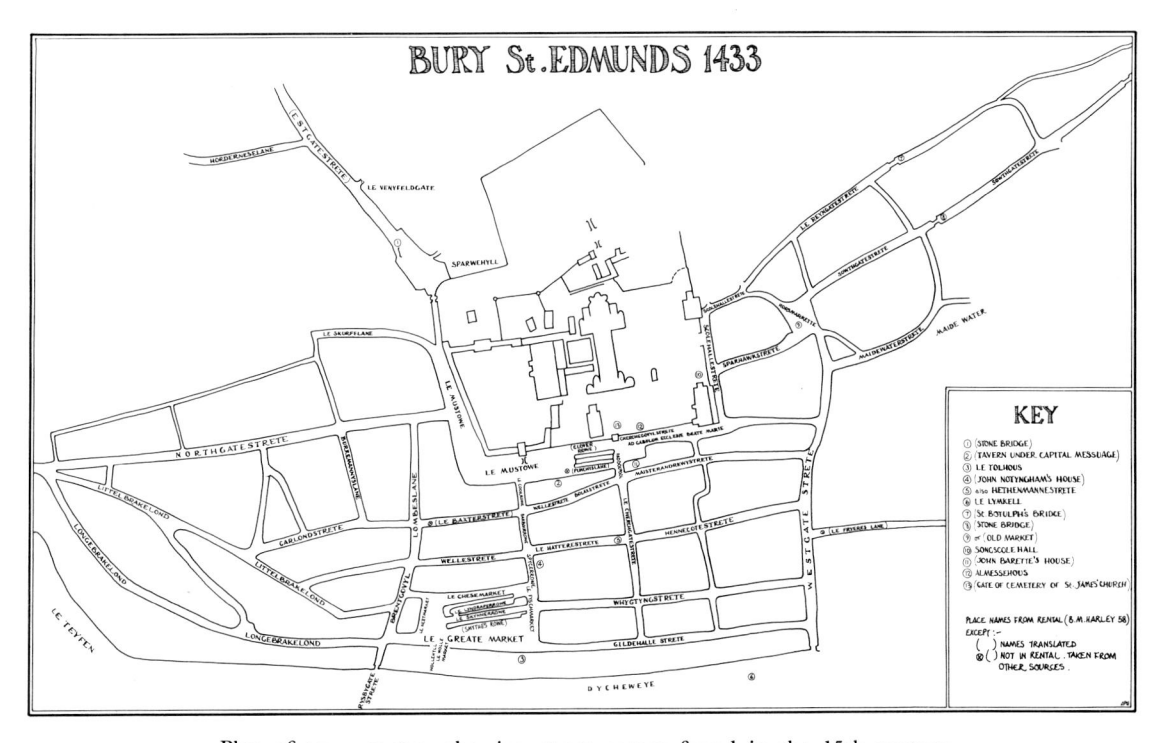

Plan of town centre, showing street names found in the 15th century.

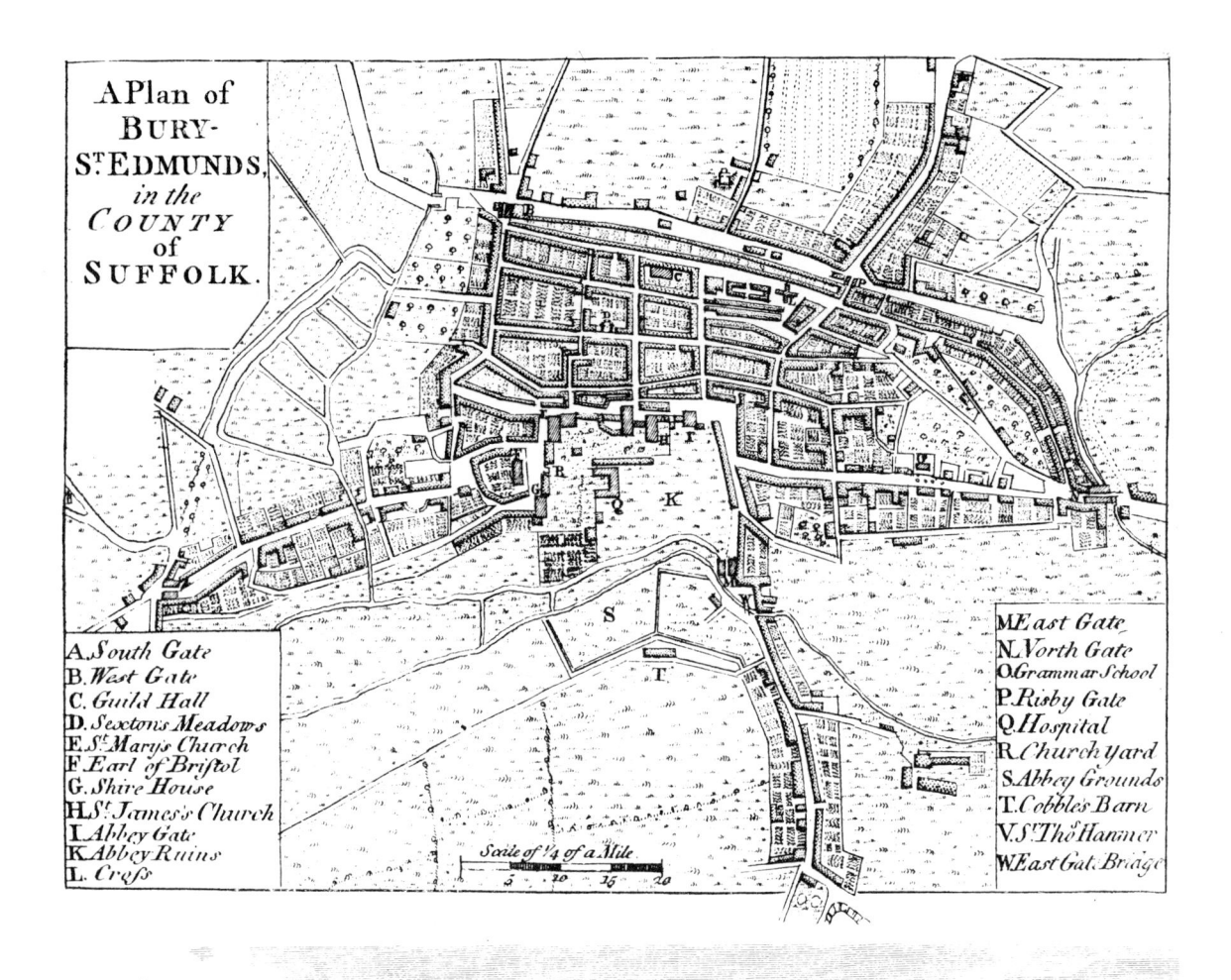

ABOVE: A small version of Downing's map, 1740. (JK) BELOW: The Eastgate Gate stood between the Abbot's Bridge and the Fox Inn, both of which have survived. The river was usually forded, the bridge being used by pedestrians and in times of flood. The building above the river was used as an almshouse in 1612. (JK)

LEFT: The North Gate, with the other town gates, was demolished between 1761 and 1765. (JK) RIGHT: A stone chapel stood near the Risbygate, on the site of the Grapes Hotel. (JK) BELOW: The engraver of this view of the Abbey Gate died in 1742, and it is shown without its turrets but with damage to the corners of the building which does not seem to have been repaired until this century. The ditch is, however, shown.

LEFT: Norman workmanship is to be found in several houses other than Moyses Hall; this is the hall of 79, Guildhall Street, before the Norman work was covered up. (OGJ) RIGHT: Chequer Square, a pencil sketch by Henry Davy, 19 October 1818. The gabled building on the east corner of Athenaeum Lane is now part of the Masonic Lodge, formerly the Six Bells; the entrance to the yard was filled in within the last 30 years. Comparison with Smith's 'Norman Gateway' shows that, since 1809, the house on the other corner of the lane had been given a brick facade. (St E) OPPOSITE: Long-handled implements called cromes were used to pull burning thatch from roofs; 10s 0d was spent on repairing those belonging to the town in 1608. (SRO(B))
BELOW: Relief after disasters such as fires was raised by means of briefs read in church. A note shows that 3s 4d was collected for Bury St Edmunds at Shudy Camps in Cambridgeshire. (SRO(I))

THE
𝔚𝔬𝔢𝔣𝔲𝔩𝔩 𝔞𝔫𝔡 𝔏𝔞𝔪𝔢𝔫𝔱𝔞𝔟𝔩𝔢

wast and spoile done by a suddaine

Fire in S. Edmonds-bury in

Suffolke, on Munday, the tenth

of Aprill. 1 6 0 8.

LONDON

Printed for *Henrie Gosson*, and are to be solde in Pater-
noster rowe, *at the Signe of the Sunne*.
1 6 0 8.

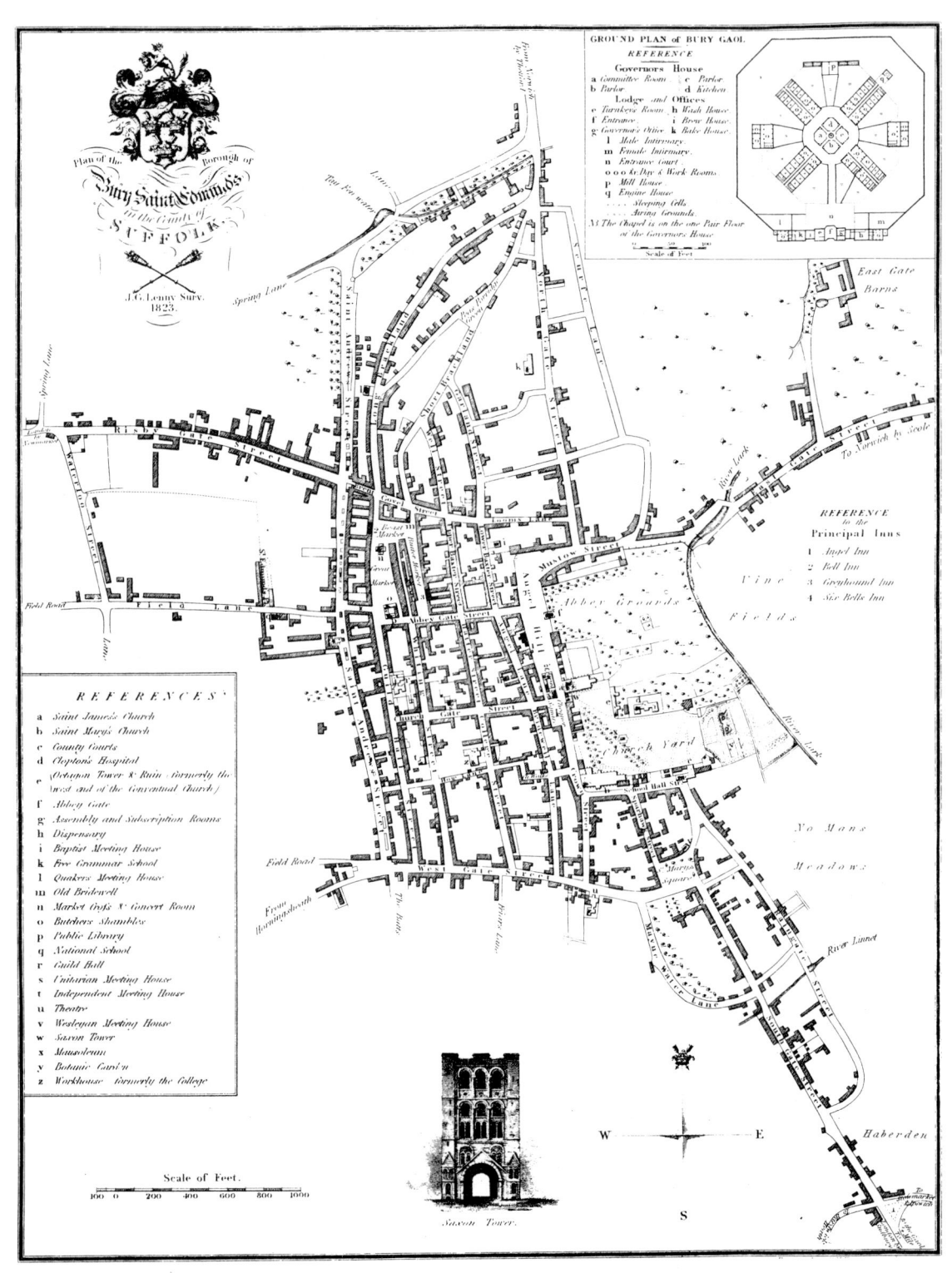

Lenny's map of Bury St Edmunds, in 1823. Hodson's first Botanic Garden
is marked in part of the precinct where the County Council Car Park is now.
(JK)

80   *Account of the Coaches, &c.*

The Distance of the Market or Post Towns, and an Account of the Coaches, &c. with their Stages to and from BURY, &c.

From Bury to	Newmarket,	14 Post Miles.
—to	Cambridge,	27
—to	Stowmarket,	14
—to	Needham,	18
—to	Ipswich,	27
—to	Ixworth,	7
—to	Botesdale,	16
—to	Thetford,	12
—to	Mildenhall,	11
—to	Sudbury,	16
—to	Lavenham,	10
—to	Hadleigh,	20
—to	Haverhill,	17

Coaches and Stages to London, Norwich, &c.

C. from the Angel-Inn, every Monday Wednesday and Friday to Green-Dragon, and Bull-Inns, Bishopgate-street, *London*, carry four Inside Passengers at 16s. each; returns Tuesdays, Thursdays, and Saturdays

C. from the Greyhound in the Butter-Market, to dit. on Tuesdays, Thursdays and Saturdays; returns Mondays, Wednesdays and Fridays, to carry six Insides, at 13s. each.

C. from

Account of the Coaches, &c.   81

C. from the Greyhound aforesaid, to the Bear-Inn at *Yarmouth*, on Tuesdays and Saturdays; returns on Mondays and Fridays, Summer and Winter: Fare, 10s.——Distance 58 Miles.

C. from the Angel in *Norwich*, to Swan with 2 Necks Lad-Lane, *London*, in one Day Summer Season, every Tuesday, Thursday and Saturday; returns on Mondays Wednesdays and Fridays; breakfasts at the Half Moon in *Bury*, going up; dines at *Botesdale* coming down; Fare from *Norwich* to *London*, 1l. 8s. from *Norwich* to *Bury*, 10s. from *Bury* to *London*, 15s. Winter Season, in a Day and half, Coaches meet and lie at *Bury*; to carry 6 Inside Passengers. Fare from *Norwich* to *London*, 25s. to *Bury*, and from thence to *London* as above.

Chaise from Mr. Revett's opposite the North-gate-street, to *Ipswich*, every Tuesday, returns the following Day: Insides, 6s. outsides, 3s.

Chaise from the Red Hart in *Cambridge*, to White Horse *Bury*, every Monday and Friday, returns to *Cambridge* on Tuesdays and Saturdays. Fare 7s. ——by BARKER.

Cart from *Haverhill*, to the Griffin-Inn, *Bury*, every Tuesday, returns Wednesday Morning.——WEBB.

Cart from *Bildiston*, to the Red Lyon in *Bury*, every Friday, returns on Saturdays, by way of *Lavenham*.

M   Caravan

ABOVE: This print of passengers going to Bury Fair was made in 1770, by which time there were regular coach services to London and other towns, with carts and waggons to most villages. (St E) BELOW: Coach services listed in *A Description of Bury St Edmunds*, 1771. (SRO(B))

ABOVE: In 1890 the Eastern Counties Navigation and Transport Co Ltd extended the Lark Navigation from Fornham St Martin into the town, to a point near the Keymarket store in Mildenhall Road. Some Directors, including the 3rd Marquess of Bristol (in top hat) are on a barge at the opening ceremony. (OGJ) BELOW: Part of the title page of the Act for making the Lark navigable 1699; this copy belonged to Thomas Macro, who built Cupola House, and was Coroner (immediate past Alderman) when the act was passed. (SRO(I))

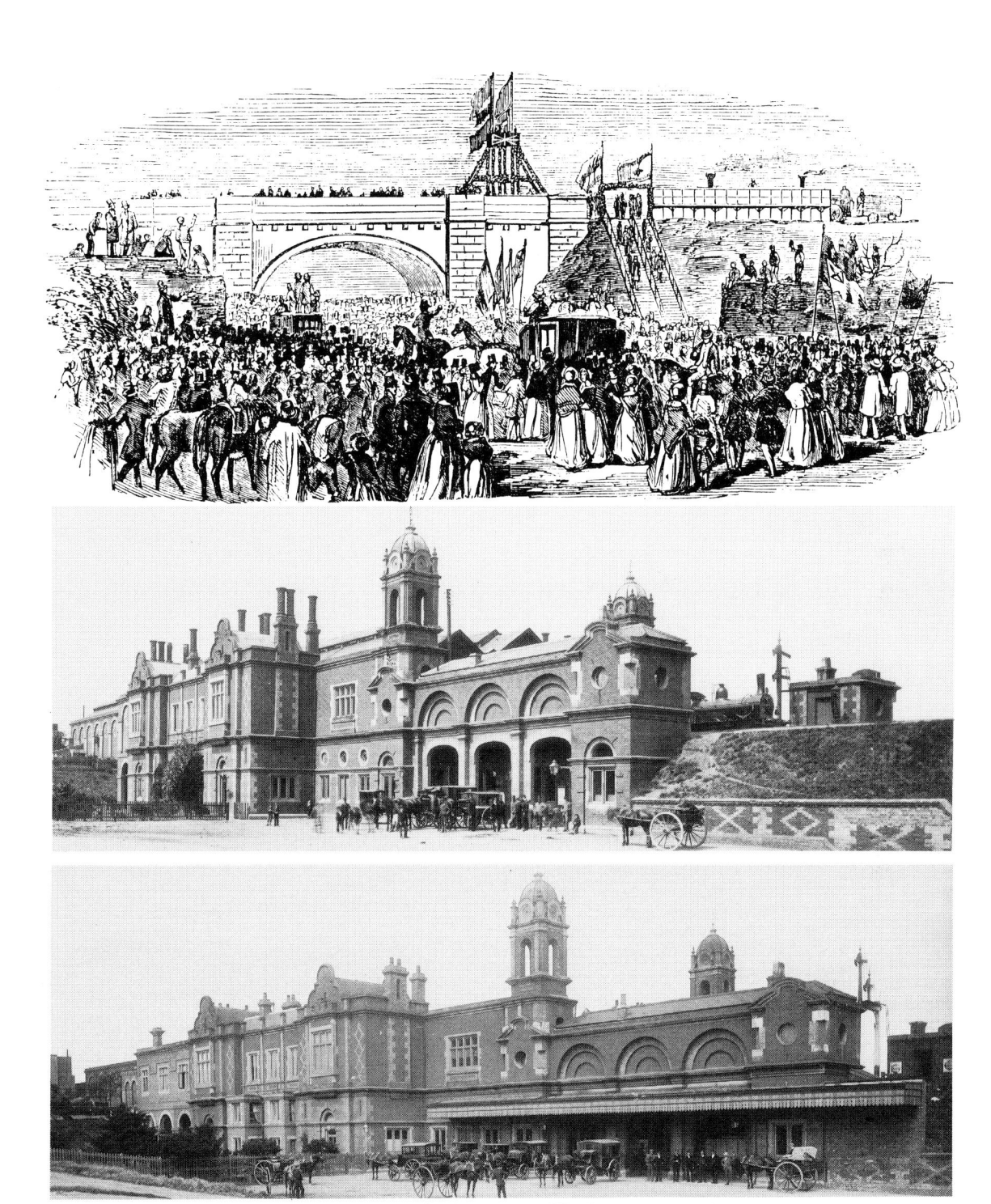

ABOVE: Opening of the Bury and Ipswich Railway, 1846. The Directors and the Mayor and Corporation of Ipswich arrived by special train and were welcomed on a special platform set up on the Ipswich side of the viaduct, before processing into the town for a banquet in the Concert Room (Market Cross). Mr Gurdon, the Recorder, said that the price of coal had fallen by 10% to 15% on the day the first coal train had arrived. (SRO(B)) CENTRE: Northgate Station, about 1873. The steam engine is a 'Little Sharpie', a type introduced in 1867. (OGJ) BELOW: Northgate Station after the destruction of the glass roof over the platforms in 1893. A canopy had been provided at the front. (OGJ)

24

Relics of Renown

Bede tells in his *History of the English Church and People* how Sigeberht, king of the East Angles in about 630, renounced his throne and retired to a monastery which he had founded, entrusting his kingdom to his brother Ecgric. His intention of spending the rest of his life as a religious came to nothing when the heathen Mercians, under their king, Penda, invaded the East Anglian Kingdom; to encourage his people, Sigeberht was forcibly dragged from the monastery to lead them against the invaders. Armed with nothing more than a stick, Sigeberht died in this battle. The Ely tradition, preserved in *Liber Eliensis*, states that Sigeberht's monastery was at *Bedricesworth*, which later became Bury St Edmunds. Sigeberht's Royal foundation and his associations with this place explain why the town was later regarded as a *villa regia*, a Royal town, and why it was chosen as the burial place of another, more famous king of the East Angles.

That Edmund, king of the East Angles, is a shadowy figure, about whom we know with certainty no more than that he was killed by the invading Danes in 869. As his principal feast was from an early date celebrated on 20 November, that is almost certainly the anniversary of his death. A large body of legend soon grew up about the life of Edmund. Some episodes recorded by his biographers were portrayed in illuminations, stained glass and on carvings — one favourite incident is the discovery of his head carefully guarded by a ferocious wolf, which was the crest of the borough of Bury St Edmunds from 1606 until 1974, and since then has been used as the crest of the St Edmundsbury Borough Council.

The earliest evidence of Edmund's fame as a saint is the remarkable series of pennies known as the St Edmund memorial coinage. These circulated even in the Danelaw—those parts of the country governed by the Danes before the death of Alfred the Great in 899, and almost certainly before the Canterbury mint ceased production in 892, indicating that Edmund was venerated as a saint within 30 years of death and probably sooner. Possibly Edmund was regarded as a 'resistance leader' against the Danes, though it hardly helps to understand why the coins were current in the Danelaw.

Controversy will no doubt continue about the site of King Edmund's martyrdom. His earliest biographer, Abbo, writing between 985 and 987, placed it at *Haegelisdun*, the old name for Hellesdon, and it has been suggested that the place of that name on the outskirts of Norwich might be the site. If that were so, it seems strange the body was not interred at Norwich. Archdeacon Hermann, the first Bury St Edmunds writer to describe St Edmund's death, does not say where he was killed but that he was first buried at Sutton. This statement has sometimes led to the questionable conclusion that the ancient Royal burial place of Sutton Hoo was defiantly re-used. Then recently in the course of discussion with Miss Mavis Baker, an enthusiastic field walker, Dr Stanley West noticed a field-name, Hellesdon, on the (admittedly 19th century) Bradfield St Clare tithe map. *Valor Ecclesiasticus* shows that the Cellarer of the Abbey of St Edmund paid 6s 8d to the hall of Bradfield St Clare and 3s 4d to Sutton Hall in the same parish. Unless Bradfield St Clare had been a place of special importance to the Abbey, these payments are quite inexplicable and, in addition, in the neighbouring parish of Rougham, Royal connections may be indicated by the

OPPOSITE ABOVE: Eastgate Station was the terminus for trains to and from Sudbury from 1865 until 1909, and had been demolished before 1924. It was on the south side of Eastgate Street, near the fly-over. (SRO(B))
CENTRE: As railway travel became usual, the inns ceased to be the termini of journeys and the more substantial hotels provided omnibuses to take guests to and from the station. The coach in the foreground going towards St John's Street is the Suffolk Hotel omnibus, 1868. (SRO(B)) BELOW: This aerial photograph, taken in 1976, illustrates the size of the precinct and the puzzling irregularities of the so-called grid of streets. It is easy to see that Northgate Street and Sparhawk Street are on the same line. (SAU)

place name Kingshall, the king's hill. Furthermore, one of the open fields of Rougham was called St Edmund's field, and a fifteenth century terrier mentions a St Edmund's watering place; whether St Edmund's Hill, the name by which Professor Symonds called his Adam house and estate on the hill east of Bury St Edmunds, was old or invented by him has still to be determined. What is certain is that *Haegelisdun*, which would become the modern place name Hellesdon, could never develop into Hoxne. Probably the supposition that that was the site of St Edmund's martyrdom was fostered by the Bishops of Norwich, whose manor it was, in the hope of diverting some of the offerings lavished onto St Edmund into their own coffers, after their attempts to establish the East Anglian See at Bury St Edmunds had failed.

Eventually, some time in the early years of the tenth century, St Edmund's body was brought from the place where it was first buried to *Bedricesworth*, and a simple wooden church, perhaps similar to that which still survives at Greenstead in Essex, housed the saint's body.. Abbo's account suggests that it was necessary to build a church to receive St Edmund's body, which in turn suggests that Sigeberht's church, or its successor, had been destroyed by the Danes, or was considered unworthy for its new function. The shrine was not then cared for by monks but by secular clergy, ie clergy who went out from their church — probably a minster church — serving the spiritual needs of those who lived in the surrounding countryside.

From 1010 until 1014, *Bedricesworth* was so much at risk from further attack by the Danes that, for the sake of safety, St Edmund's body was taken to London; it was returned when the danger passed. During that journey his body rested at Greenstead. Such was the saint's influence that a Royal grant had been made to him of the land surrounding his shrine, and those who lived in this privileged area, the *banleuca*, made payment to the saint when the men of the shire paid geld to the Crown. Not surprisingly, when Swegn Forkbeard died, shortly after he had tried to force those who lived within the four crosses to pay him geld, it was generally believed that St Edmund was responsible. His son Cnut, anxious to placate the vengeful saint, established Benedictine monks at *Bedricesworth*, the first members of the community coming, half from St Benet's Hulme in the parish of Horning near Norwich, and half from Ely; they brought with them half the possessions of those houses. A round, stone church was soon built on part of the site where the Lady Chapel later stood, and it was consecrated in 1032. After that *Bedricesworth* faded in favour of place-names of which St Edmund was an element.

The Abbey church, of which the ruins are still to be seen, was begun by Abbot Baldwin, the Frenchman appointed in 1065, whose favour with William the Conqueror ensured that Bury St Edmunds prospered in the years after the Conquest. As well as encouraging both French and Englishmen to settle here, Baldwin began to build the Abbey church; by 1097, the eastern part was sufficiently advanced for dedication and for the body of St Edmund to be translated from Cnut's round church. After Baldwin's death in 1097, building lost momentum, until Abbot Anselm, who ruled from 1121-1148, took up the work with renewed vigour and enlarged Baldwin's plan for the Abbey church and precinct.

The surviving remains of the Abbey church do little to illustrate either its size or the quality of its workmanship, which can be deduced from accounts of the building and from the few remaining fragments. A plan or an aerial photograph shows how small the cathedral is compared with the Abbey church and, before the new Cathedral choir was built, it would have been possible to stand St James's and St Mary's churches inside the abbey church, end to end, and still have space to spare. The two surviving gateways, the Church or Cemetery Gate, now called the Norman Tower, and the Court Gate, now called the Abbey Gate, are the only buildings to survive anything like intact. The two churches stand within the precinct and, before the dissolution, there were also within its walls several chapels to be seen, as well as all the domestic buildings of the Abbey community.

Within the precinct by the Abbey Gate, were, immediately to its left, the stable and the offices of the master of the horse and, following the wall which goes along Mustow Street, the cowshed, brewery, bakery, mill and granary which served the convent. At right angles to them, on the site of the present house, were the Abbot's stable, bakery and brewery; the Abbot's household was run independently and, during a vacancy, the endowments set aside for his establishment were taken by the Crown. Across the precinct, the Abbot's palace came next, followed by special accommodation for the many Royal visitors, while beyond them to the east, near the river, was the Abbot's garden. One of its corners, marked by a dovecote, is still easily distinguished. The monks' dormitory was above the buildings which adjoined the chapter house and nearby, to the east, were the bath and reredorter, a monastic cloakroom. Along the north side of the cloister was the refectory, in which Parliament met on more than one occasion. North and west of the refectory were the kitchens and store rooms in which the Cellarer kept food stocks, while to the west again was the Abbot's hall of pleas in which he held his court. Beyond the river Lark was the vineyard while, on the south side of the precinct, there was the Abbey song school, abutting on the east end of St Mary's Church, and the grammar school on the site of Shire Hall. In monastic times there were a number of free-standing chapels within the precinct. Some have disappeared without trace above ground, such as the two dedicated to St John. One, known as St John-at-the-Hill, stood near St Mary's, just within the precinct wall in Crown Street, and the other, St John at the Well *(ad fontem)*, may be the chapel referred to in a deed of Abbot Samson, which was to be built between the West Front and the Norman Tower. It is believed that fragments of the chapel of St Margaret have been found, in the course of alterations to the house of that name which adjoins Shire Hall, while the Chapel of the Charnel still remains a feature of the churchyard. It was founded in about 1300 by Abbot John of Northwold, to provide a seemly resting place for bones from earlier burials, which were disturbed in the course of digging new graves. Comings and goings would have been unceasing; pilgrims, great officers of state, merchants of all kinds, as well as poor folk from round about must have thronged in and out through the Abbey Gate. Some say that a group of barons met here in 1214 to settle the terms of the Magna Carta, but the Abbey's own records are silent on this point, and this incident, if it took place, has been given far too much attention in recent years, at the expense of well-authenticated and more directly relevant events.

The Abbey church was built on the lines of the great pilgrimage churches of the continent. The apsidal east end afforded an ambulatory for pilgrims to move round the huge building, without impeding the monks as they went about the service of the church in the choir. At the heart of it all was the shrine of St Edmund, shimmering with silver gilt and precious stones. If the Abbey was at the heart of mediaeval Bury St Edmunds, the shrine of St Edmund was at the heart of the Abbey church. People came from all over England, and even farther afield, to worship there.

The Abbot of St Edmunds was not merely the father and pastor of the community which lived within this large but enclosed area of Bury St Edmunds for, in addition to his monastic position, he ranked as one of the great magnates of the realm. The Abbot was lord of the town of Bury St Edmunds, and held responsible by the King if his subordinates failed in their duties. Throughout the Liberty of St Edmund, a large part of the county identical to the area later to be administered by the old West Suffolk County Council, the Abbot's courts regulated many aspects of life. On a national level, the Abbot had his seat as a peer in Parliament, and provided knights to fight for the King in time of war, as any other magnate would do. The fame of St Edmund ensured that pilgrims thronged to the shrine, making their offerings to the saint. There is little wonder that first Bishop Herfast between 1071 and 1081, and then Herbert de Losinga in 1101/2, attempted to settle the East Anglian See at Bury St Edmunds, which would have diverted some of the wealth of the Abbey to the Bishopric. It was in the course of these disputes that Abbot Baldwin obtained exemption from episcopal jurisdiction, which placed the town as well as the Abbey apart from the Diocese of Norwich.

Mediaeval buildings were not always so solid as they looked and here, as elsewhere, towers fell and fire damaged or destroyed buildings; indeed, building activity can hardly ever have ceased.

To take but one instance, a major disaster took place in 1465 when some workmen were repairing the western tower, which had fallen in two stages in 1430 and 1431. Off they went for their lunch, leaving a brazier alight in the tower. Soon fire had spread all along the wooden roof of the nave, and there is a splendid account of how the wooden lantern gently fell down inside the central tower it had once surmounted.

Everyone interested in the Abbey of St Edmund ought to read the *Chronicle of Jocelin of Brakelond*, which gives a rare and privileged view of monastic life. Abbot Hugh had been weak, and allowed the Abbey to fall into debt. His successor, the famous Abbot Samson, set himself to reform the abuses which he found on his succession, and to pay off those debts. Jocelin illustrates the reaction of the monks to this strong and, at times, rather arrogant and overbearing administrator. In addition to its main theme, his *Chronicle* affords glimpses of life in Abbey and town. One of the fires which were all too apt to devastate buildings in mediaeval times occurred during Samson's time, and Jocelin records how the Abbot and a few of the monks examined St Edmund's body for damage, and found that his nose was very large! Samson's wise and moderate attitude to the townsmen is shown by his reaction when festivities in the churchyard on 'boxing day' got out of hand. The Abbot punished all those responsible, being especially severe with his own servants but, once the wrong-doers had been punished, resumed the usual practice of entertaining townsmen at his table for the twelve days of Christmas, although entertainments in the churchyard (whatever they may have been) were henceforth forbidden.

Few of the works of art which were once in the Abbey have survived. The bronze doors of Master Hugo must have been destroyed at the dissolution, and debate continues about the possible Bury provenance of the ivory cross in the Metropolitan Museum in New York. The Bury Bible in Corpus Christi College, Cambridge, is without doubt the work of Master Hugo, and demonstrates the artistic achievement of the Abbey at the height of its fame.

Soon after the dissolution the Abbey site was sold, and remained entirely in lay ownership until quite recently. The Abbot's Palace became a private house until it was demolished in 1720, and it was probably in that part of the Abbey that Thomas Badby, who then owned the site, entertained Queen Elizabeth I when she visited Bury St Edmunds, in the course of her progress through Suffolk in 1578. There is evidence that some, perhaps all, of the west front had been converted into houses by the Restoration and, a little later, the Jesuit mission to Suffolk was using part as headquarters. A deed of 1749 shows that by then Samson's tower and the adjacent part of the West Front were the stables of the Six Bells Inn (now Masonic Lodge), but that before then it had been a private house, and then the Assembly House stables. In 1848 the stables were sold by auction for £520, to be converted into a dye works, a letter to the local press suggesting that they should be bought and adapted as a residence for the Mayor for the time being presumably having failed to gain support. They acquired their present form in the spring of 1863, when they were converted into the Bury St Edmunds Probate Registry.

The monastic grammar school was conveyed to the Guildhall Feoffees in 1578 as the Shire House or Hall, and may well have been adapted before then; it has been rebuilt many times and it is doubtful whether any of the mediaeval work remains. For a time in the 17th century the Chapel of the Charnel was a public house and later a blacksmith's house and shop. Eventually it was acquired by John Spink, a local banker, who converted it into a family mausoleum. It was his intention to give the churchyard, which he owned, to the Corporation, and he had his portrait (now in the Guildhall) painted, holding the conveyance. Unfortunately, his bank failed before he was able to do this, but in 1798 it was bought by another prominent Bury banker, James Oakes, who almost immediately conveyed it to the Corporation, who remain its owners to this day. In 1953, they also bought the Abbey Gardens and the West Front, thus becoming the corporate owner of much of the former precinct, the rest of it belonging to the County Council and the ecclesiastical authorities.

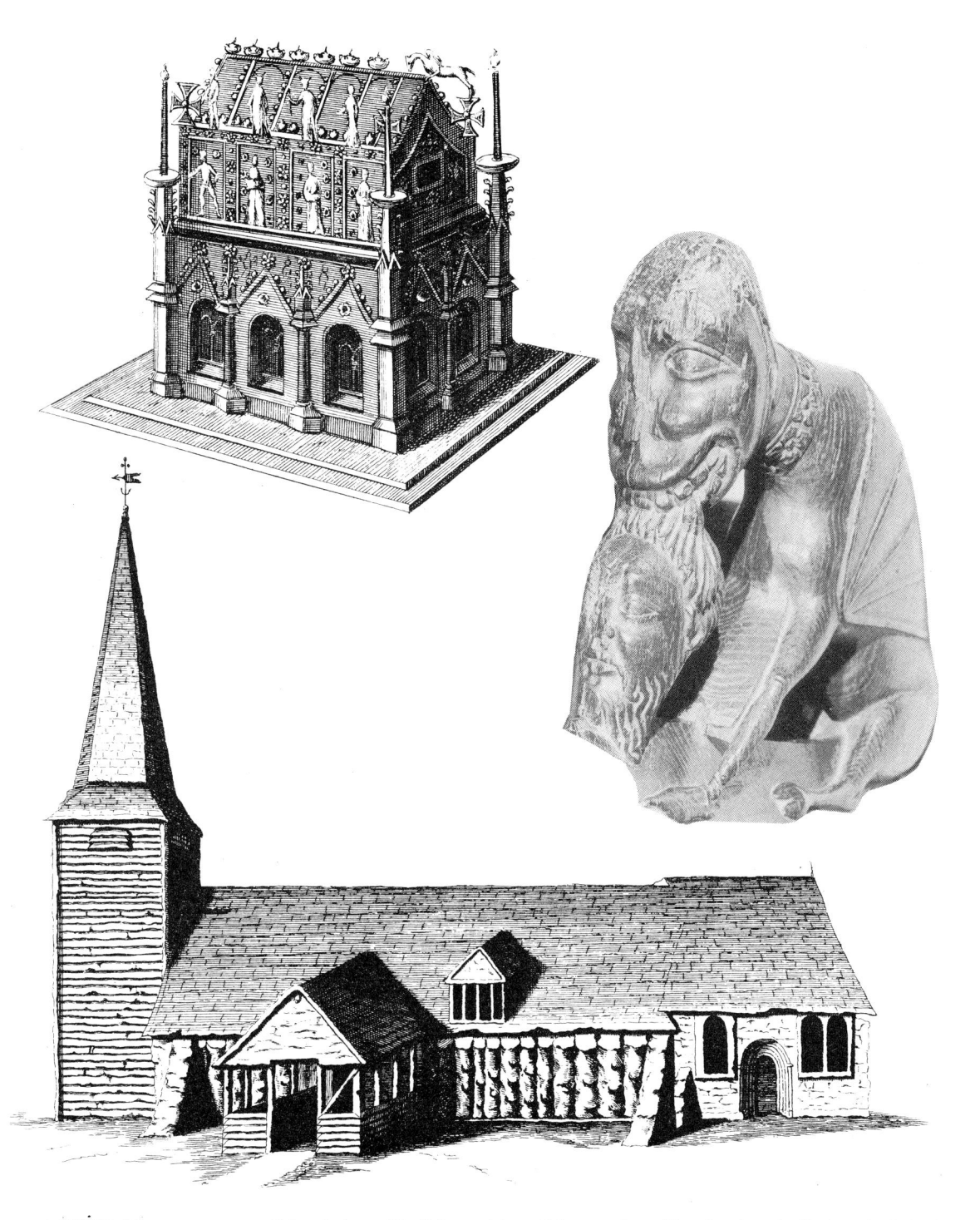

LEFT: The appearance of the shrine of St Edmund is well known from illuminations in Lydgate's *Life of St Edmund*, on which this engraving is based. It was covered with plates of silver gilt, and jewels offered at the shrine were hung upon it. (JK) RIGHT: Bench end in Hadleigh Church with carving of the wolf holding St Edmund's head. (JA) BELOW: Greenstead Church; St Edmund's body is supposed to have rested here on its return from London in 1010. The early church buildings here may have looked like this. (JK)

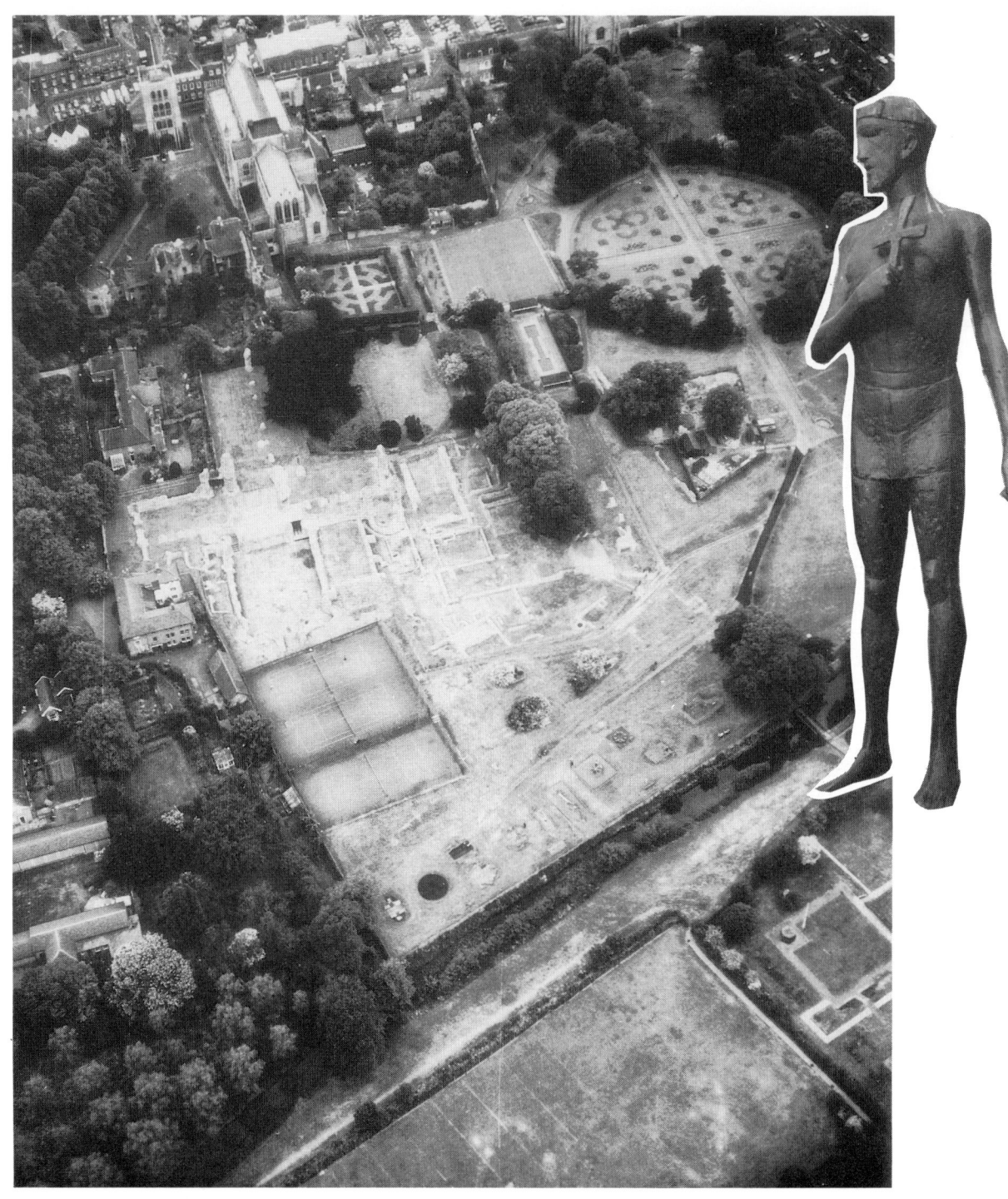

Part of the precinct from the air. The west front of the Abbey is only a few feet east of the Cathedral as extended, while the easternmost apse is under the first tennis court. The parch marks show the position of the walls of buildings not yet excavated. (SAU) INSET: St Edmund, by Dame Elizabeth Frink, commissioned by the West Suffolk County Council to mark the end of the Liberty of St Edmund as an administrative unit, 1974. (HCS)

LEFT: Skeletons of five of the Abbots of St Edmund revealed in the Chapter House on New Year's Day, 1903. From the front they are Edmund of Walpole (1248-1256), Henry of Rushbrook (1235-1248), Richard of the Isle (of Ely)(1229-1234), Samson (1182-1211) and Ording (1148-1157). (OGJ)
BELOW: Godfrey's print of 1779 shows the Norman Tower with its tympanum still in place, cupola on top, and clock dial. Note sculpture in panel on left of arch. (JK) RIGHT: Drawing, undated, showing the tympanum in some detail. From the accounts given when it was removed in 1789, it was probably not part of the original. (SRO(B))

ABOVE: The carving of the two devils casting a man into hell, removed from a side panel of the Norman Tower, is now in Moyses Hall; it was probably originally part of the west door of the Abbey church. (SRO(B))
BELOW: This engraving of the sculpture shows how it has deteriorated in the last two centuries. (JK)
RIGHT: Davy's engraving of 1820 is one of the many views which left out the cupola, which was removed in 1845. The ground round the tower was excavated to its original level but the battlements were not replaced when the tower was restored. (JK)

ABOVE LEFT: Davy's companion view from the east, 1820. (JK) RIGHT: The Norman Tower photographed c1945, when this part of the churchyard still looked like one. (RWE) BELOW LEFT: An engraving of the Abbey Gate before its stair turrets were removed early in the 18th century from Battley's *Antiquitates*, sets the turrets away from the corners. Some prints and all photographs taken before c1912 show damage to the corners, perhaps the result of the fall of the turrets. RIGHT: Whittock's engraving of the Abbey Gate from the west, c1840. The railings first appear about 1840 and may date from 1831, when Hodson opened his Botanic Garden in what had been the Great Court. (JK)

ABOVE: The West Front, engraved from a drawing made in 1680, shows how houses had already been built into the ruins. Note the cupola on the Norman Tower. (JK) BELOW: An engraving of a drawing by John King which illustrated his paper on the abbey in *Archaeologia*, vol III (1786), which shows the west front as it was in his day with post-dissolution buildings added, with his impression of its probable appearance had those buildings not been inserted. (JK)

ABOVE: Kendall's engraving of the West Front, 1787. Samson's Tower was already a stable, there were two houses, but no buildings in the part now called the Courtyard. (St E) CENTRE: In the spring of 1863, Samson's Tower and adjacent parts of the West Front were altered to form a Probate Registry and Registrar's residence. Before then, this part of the west front had been a dye-works and, earlier still, stables. William Rednall was the architect. (SRO(B)) BELOW: This drawing and that of the Abbot's Bridge were made by Francis Grose for his *Antiquarian Repository* in 1777. Here Samson's Tower is shown thatched, as it remained until it became the Probate Registry; the Chapel of the Charnel was still a private house, and Grose has faithfully reproduced the cupola which surmounted the Norman Tower until 1845. (JK)

ABOVE: Although published only nine years after Grose made his drawing, Kendall's engraving of 1786 shows the Chapel of the Charnel as a ruin. (SRO(B)) BELOW: Grose's view of the Abbot's Bridge, which is really a continuation of the precinct wall across the river. (JK)

ABOVE: Abbot's Palace in 1720, before it was demolished by Major Richardson Pack. LEFT: The house in the foreground right is that known as Alwyne House, which stands on the site of the Abbot's granary etc. (St E) RIGHT: An initial from the Bury St Edmunds Psalter showing the Son and the Father, with a dove between them. They are surrounded by angels and beneath their feet are two black devils in chains. It illustrates the BCP Psalm 110, 'The Lord said unto my Lord: Sit thou on my right hand, until I make thine enemies thy footstool'. (SRO(B)) BELOW: Those who only know the Abbey site as it is now will scarcely recognise this view of the choir altar site taken in the 1950s when it was known as the wilderness. (SRO(B))

ABOVE: George Quinton's water colour of 1804 shows that by then the Linnet and the Lark joined at the end of the garden of Abbey Precincts, as they do now. Remains of a stone bridge, shown here on the left, are to be seen in several prints. (SRO(B)) BELOW: So little remains of the Abbey that several attempts have been made at conjectural reconstructions. Cottingham's, dating from the 1850s, only shows the churches and the Norman Tower. He does not show the houses which had been built under the abbey wall, or the ditch which was in front of these buildings. The continuous line of the abbey wall shown here reminds us that originally the precinct, including the Great Churchyard, was totally enclosed. (OGJ)

ABOVE: Arthur Lankester's drawing of 1875 attempts a reconstruction of the scene in 1415, although the present nave of St James's Church, begun in 1503, is shown. (OGJ) BELOW: W.K. Hardy's picture, drawn in 1883, is useful in demonstrating the enormous size of the Abbey church compared with the two parish churches, both of which are of considerable size. (OGJ)

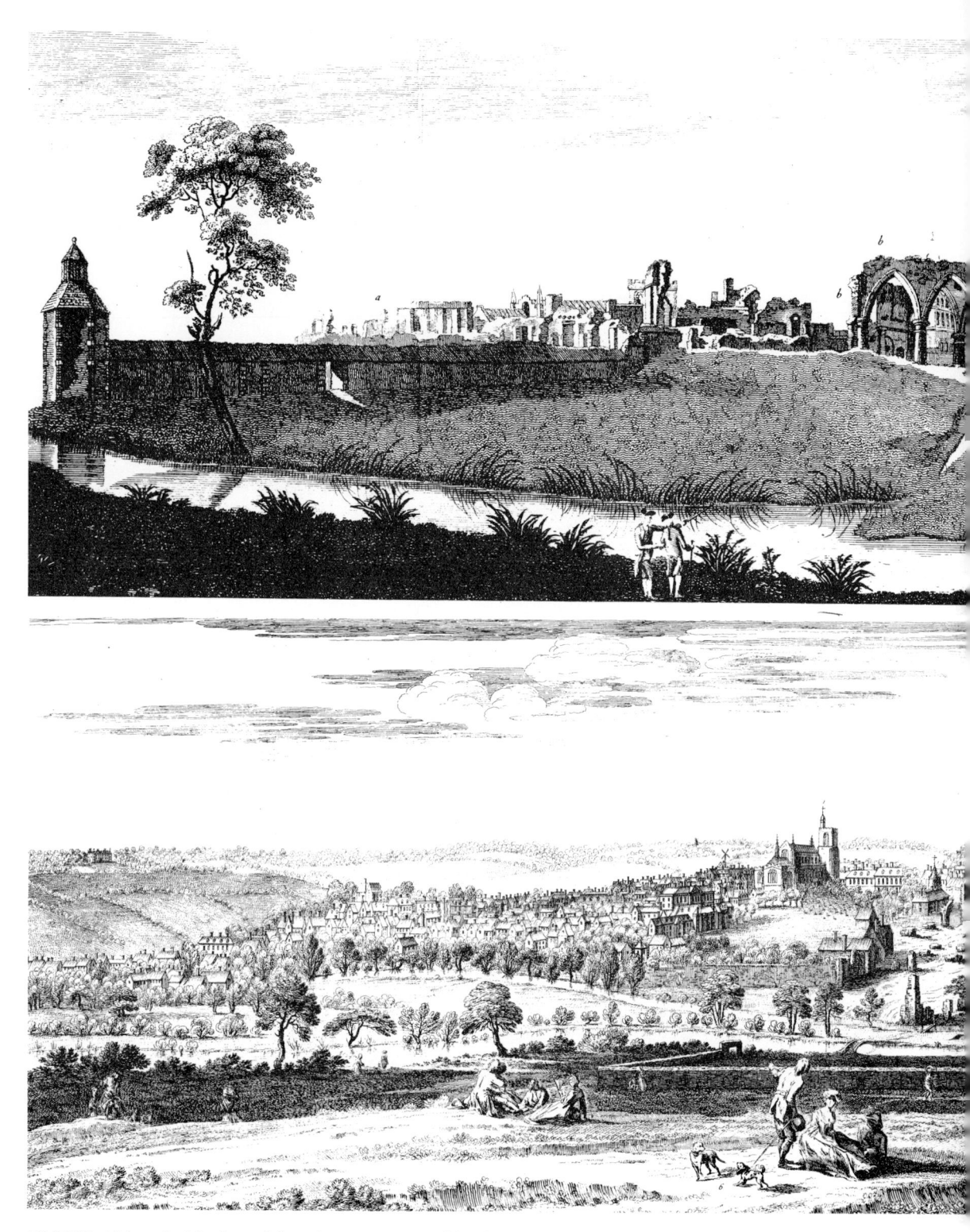

ABOVE: Although this view of the ruins was engraved by Godfrey in 1779, the drawing on which it was based was made c1725 and shows parts of the transept, chapter house, dormitory, King's hall and mill still standing.

BELOW: The East prospect by S. and N. Buck published in 1741 suggests that a great deal was lost in the 1720s and 1730s.

41

217 Feet

ABOVE: Warren's engraving of the south side of St Mary's Church, in 1747, shows the south porch, demolished in 1831 and removed to Nowton Court. BELOW: Godfrey's engraving, 1779, shows the Church still with turret for the clock bell, but ignores the buildings adjoining the Church on the north. (JK)

The Ways of the Lord

Both ancient parish churches stand within the precinct of the Abbey of St Edmund which, before the dissolution in 1539, would not have lain within either parish. The boundary between St Mary's and St James's ran along the middle of Abbeygate Street, with the south side of the street and the southern part of the town, including St Mary's Square (the pre-Conquest market place), in St Mary's parish, while St James's parish included the present enormous market place, which was part of the Norman town plan.

The Sacrist of St Edmund's was considered the parson of both Bury parishes throughout the monastic period. He took all fees from the two churches, and appointed parochial chaplains for each church who were responsible for services and pastoral care within the parish. The first Ministers' Account of the Abbey's possessions after dissolution shows that any profit, after the Sacrist had met the expenses of running St James's Church, was applied to the use of the monastery guest house. As the Abbey was exempt from episcopal jurisdiction, so were the two churches, the Sacrist having responsibility for the major functions normally carried out by the Archdeacon. After the dissolution, when the two churches were granted to the Corporation in 1614, a clause in the charter gave to the Corporation those rights which the Abbot of St Edmund's had enjoyed on the day of dissolution. The Corporation was thus able to claim episcopal exemption for its churches, and the town clergy were not instituted by the Bishop and inducted by the Archdeacon in the usual way, until an order in Council of 1844 at last settled Bury St Edmunds as part of Thingoe Deanery and the Archdeaconry of Sudbury. Until then, the only evidence of the appointment of the town clergy is in the minute books of the Corporation.

St Mary's Church is the successor of that founded by Sigeberht in the 7th century; in the early days there would have been a wooden building. Whether or not it was ever replaced by a stone church, by the time of Robert II (1102—1107) or Anselm (1121—1148) it had to be demolished to make way for the building of the *dextram brachiam*, the right arm, of the Abbey church. To replace this building, Anselm ordered his Sacrists to build a church on the present site, in the south west corner of the precinct.

The earliest part of St Mary's Church is the centre of the chancel, with its waggon roof painted with all manner of subjects, sacred and secular, and beneath it, as a frieze, painted verses from the *Te Deum*. These are cut off abruptly at the chancel arch, indicating that, before 15th century alterations, the words continued across the west end of the chancel. Local wills show that a new tower was contemplated in 1393, that it was under construction between 1395 and 1403, and stands east of the precinct wall, indicating that the present nave is longer than its predecessor. The first bequest towards building the nave was made in 1424, with several more in 1425. No doubt the work was so organised that the church could be used as long as possible, but it was inevitable that, in the course of a major re-building, the congregation sometimes had to worship elsewhere. Parishioners used the space under the west tower of the Abbey church while their own was being rebuilt in 1430; when the great bell tower fell they had a narrow escape, as the southern part collapsed soon after one of their services ended. A bequest for a new rood loft in 1436 indicates that the new nave was then being furnished.

No-one yet knows who gave the magnificent roof, with angels in procession at the mass of Our Lady, but one strong candidate has to be John Baret, whose will of 1463 is a mine of information about his own chantry chapel, and other features of the church. His motto, 'Grace me govern', is on the angels of the canopy (which here, as in many Suffolk churches, were richly coloured), a sure sign that he was responsible. Perhaps he gave the roof during his lifetime, a possibility all the more likely since there is a roof with a similar but simpler procession in Rougham church, the parish whence came Baret's wife, Elizabeth Drury. It would be quite in keeping for this cultivated man, whose will makes clear his marked devotion to the Virgin Mary, to be the donor.

When John Baret made his will the eastern bay of the south nave aisle was the Lady Chapel, and it also contained the altar of St Martin, but the possibility of demolishing the vestry adjoining the chancel to build a chapel to match the north chancel chapel was under consideration. Baret's cadaver monument, which was intended to remind him and others of the frailty of human life and the inevitability of death, had already been made in his lifetime, and has a sculpture of him on one of the panels of the present north side. Much of the decoration of the chapel described in the will has now been lost, but the roof, which survives, shows its quality. In his will, John Baret said that he had had prepared three mirrors to be placed in the three vaults above his grave, which could, with other features which have not survived, be put into place by Henry Peyntour. In the course of the restoration of this roof by Jan Kurske in 1968 a piece of concave glass was found, which enabled the original star-like effect to be re-created. These stars, twinkling on a sunny day, are one of the glories of Bury St Edmunds.

Another feature which demonstrates the quality of craftsmanship in mediaeval Bury St Edmunds is the Nottyngham porch. John Nottyngham, an Abbeygate Street grocer who died in 1440, left money for south and west porches for St Mary's. It is not known whether a west porch was built, but the north porch, with its inscription exhorting prayers for John Nottyngham and his wife, can still be seen. In addition to the carving on the exterior, which is in need of conservation, there is a circular pendant in its ceiling, depicting God surrounded by angels.

The last phase of the 15th century rebuild was the chancel aisles or chapels and the sacrarium, which were built at the expense of John, commonly called Jankyn, Smyth, the most outstanding benefactor of Bury St Edmunds, who died in 1481; a brass to him and his wife Anne is within the altar rails of the Lady Chapel.

Over the centuries, the fabric of St Mary's has been altered in many ways, and the Church is fortunate in having a long series of prints, paintings and photographs, which chart many of the features which have come and gone over the last few centuries. Clive Paine has painstakingly recorded all the nineteenth and twentieth century changes in his recent guide book.

St James's Church, which became the Cathedral church of the new Diocese of St Edmundsbury and Ipswich in 1914, also replaced an earlier church, demolished to make way for the more grandiose scheme for the Abbey church adopted under Anselm. Abbot Baldwin (1065—1097) had built a church dedicated to St Denis, the patron saint of France and of the monastery in Paris where he had taken his monk's vows, as a parish church for those whom he had encouraged to settle in the town. By Abbot Anselm's time, (1121—1148) the Church of St Denis was found to be in the way of the north-west tower of the Abbey church, which balanced Samson's tower on the south side of the west front. In this case, the new church, which was dedicated to St James because Anselm had intended to make a pilgrimage to the shrine of St James at Compostella, but had been persuaded that it was his duty to remain in Bury St Edmunds, was built west of the earlier foundation, traces of which were revealed by an excavation by Dr Ralegh Radford, just before work began on the new Cathedral Quire.

The present nave was begun in 1503, and on stylistic grounds can be attributed to a distinguished master mason, John Wastell, who lived in the town, and succeeded Simon Clerk as the master mason of the Abbey of St Edmund. The rebuilding of the church proceeded slowly.

Although parishioners and others contributed to the cost of the nave, the Abbot and Convent engaged those who were responsible for building it. Some years after the building of St James's nave started bequests were still being received towards the cost of the stone vault of the Abbey church, so it is likely that building work at St James's took second place. As an example of the way in which lay people contributed towards such costs, Thomas Bereve, a cloth maker, left money to glaze two windows in the church. For one at the west end he left the then large sum of £10 0s 0d. This was probably the great west window, since his bequest for glazing another, near the altar of St Thomas a Becket, a saint for whom Bereve had particular devotion, was for the much smaller sum of £3 6s 8d.

Thomas Bereve also left £13 3s 4d for paving the floor of the Church and for its 'stolyng', or seating. His final bequest suggests that, for some reason, perhaps because it was difficult to raise the required money, the Abbot and convent were considering alterations to the original plan agreed with the mason. He wished to give fifteen tons of stone for building and finishing a vice (spiral staircase) provided 'that the vice go forwards upon the seid covenaunts made on the behalf of my seid Lord and the convent or ellys not', the Abbot and Convent to be responsible for the carriage of the stone. No-one knows whether Thomas Bereve's bequest was carried out. As the Sacrist was not only the titular parson, but proved local wills and was the officer of the Abbey principally responsible for building work, he must have worked hard and successfully to ensure Bereve's bequest found its way to the Church with the minimum delay. A century which saw the dissolution of the monasteries and the break with Rome may not have been the easiest time to find money to rebuild a parish church. In the event, it was long after Thomas Bereve's death that St James's nave was finished, in 1551 (in the reign of Edward VI); there is a plaque in the Church recording that Edward VI contributed £200 0s 0d to its completion. The nave is simple, but its proportions are elegant. The western bay has more enrichment than the rest; this stands outside the precinct wall, and the first Minister's Account shows that several buildings had to be demolished to make way for it.

The chancel of St James's Church has been rebuilt three times since the nave was completed in the middle of the sixteenth century. A chancel in the classical style was built in 1711 at the expense of the Corporation, who were the lay rectors and impropriators of the benefice; then a Victorian chancel was built to the design of Sir Gilbert Scott in 1865—1869, which was itself replaced by the new quire consecrated at Michaelmas 1970.

In the years between the dissolution of the Abbey and the 1614 grant of the churches with their advowsons to the Corporation, the Feoffees of the town lands assumed control and appointed the clergy, many of whom were far from orthodox. It was then that the library in St James's Church was set up. At the time, Bury was known for the 'exercises' whereby clergy and laity joined in theological discussion, and it seems likely that the origins of the library are to be found as a resource for this weekly gathering. The earliest gifts to the library show from marks on their bindings that they were once chained, while the donors include many who were concerned with the government of the town. All those concerned in buying in Sir Robert Drury's lease of 1609 gave at least one book each to the library while, in about 1630, no less than 20 of the 24 burgesses of the Common Council and four of the twelve capital burgesses made donations. The library, like the churches, was granted to the Corporation in 1614, while in 1612 James Baxter left money from an acre of land for its repair.

Just as the churches had been firmly controlled by the Abbey before the dissolution, so the Corporation kept them firmly in their charge until 1840—1841 (when they endowed them and sold their rights of presentation). There were two clergymen appointed to each church: the Curate or Reader, who read the services, visited the sick, administered the sacraments and so on, who was given no stipend but received all the fees payable, and the Lecturer or Preacher, who was well paid, as indeed he ought to have been, for the Corporation had been granted the tithes of the town to enable them to pay the clergy adequately.

By the beginning of the 19th century, it was considered desirable to provide another Anglican church. A suggestion that the upper part of the Market Cross might be converted came to nothing, but in 1841 St John's Church, whose spire is a prominent landmark, was built to serve an area taken from St James's parish. Relief was given to St Mary's by building St Peter's Church as a chapel-of-ease in 1858, while there were also a number of mission halls in both parishes.

Non-conformity soon took hold in Bury St Edmunds, perhaps by way of reaction against the all-pervading influence of the Abbey of St Edmund. There is evidence that some of the Town's leading magistrates were zealous in their support of ministers who favoured the more radical forms of religious observance, on one occasion even punishing a clergyman who read the services from the Book of Common Prayer. The clergy appointed by the Guildhall Feoffees and the Corporation were more often than not radical in their views, and it seems certain that Archbishop Laud had misgivings about the manner in which the Corporation exercised its ecclesiastical patronage.

An Independent Church was established in Bury St Edmunds in 1648 (after a false start two years earlier), the forerunner of the United Reformed Church in Whiting Street, where there has been a chapel from about 1717. A little later, in 1672, a licence was issued authorising a Presbyterian congregation to meet in the house of Samuel Moody, which was in Abbeygate Street where Dudley's (now Jumpers') is now; among the Sessions papers at the Record Office is a lively account of a conventicle at this house being broken up by the authorities. In all probability, the Presbyterians had been worshipping 'underground' since 1662, and by 1690 they had a meeting house in Churchgate Street, probably on the site of the handsome red brick chapel which was built by the congregation in 1711, as they were so numerous that they had outgrown their earlier premises. This distinguished building, with the excellent brick work of its facade and many original fittings, has in recent years fallen into a sorry state, and it is much to be hoped that the recently announced initiative to restore it will meet with success. The plate, which was made for the chapel in 1711 by Humphrey Payne of London, is now deposited with the Corporation insignia.

In 1811, the Churchgate Street congregation split; some members joined the Independents in Whiting Street, while those who remained became Unitarians. One of those associated with this chapel was Henry Crabb Robinson (1775—1867), a friend of many of the well-known literary figures of the day. He was among the founders of London University and also of the Athenaeum Club in London which, he hoped, might help to save young men from the perils of early marriage.

The Society of Friends, perhaps better known as the Quakers, have also been established here since the 17th century. The Quaker message was first preached in the town in 1655 by George Harrison, a gentleman, who was accompanied by a farm labourer, Stephen Hubberty. In 1672, three private houses were licenced for worship for the Friends, and in 1682 they acquired a house on part of the site of the present meeting house in St John's Street. The Quakers suffered a great deal from their refusal to pay tithes and Philip Butler, a member of the Bury Meeting, was active as the Secretary of the Suffolk Tithe Payers' Association; his recollections were used by the BBC in a *Yesterday's Witness* programme.

John Wesley preached in a building in St Mary's Square, which soon became too small for the Methodist congregation, and was replaced in 1811 by a larger chapel, now a private house, 4A, St Mary's Square. By 1878, this chapel no longer sufficed for the needs of the congregation, which moved into the present building in Brentgovel Street.

Cornelius Elvin, the founder of the Garland Street Baptist Chapel, was brought up as a Congregationalist who worshipped in the Whiting Street Chapel until, as a result of his study of the scriptures, he joined an Ebenezer Baptist Chapel in Lower Baxter Street, whose burial ground still survives between the garden of 8, Angel Hill and the Borough Offices' car park. He became Pastor to this congregation in 1823 and, within a decade, the small chapel had become inadequate for the large following which had grown up following his ministry. A site was acquired in Garland Street and a chapel capable of seating 1,200 built in 1834. Elvin was liberal in his views and in 1837 those who desired a stricter form of the Baptist faith established the Rehoboth Chapel in Westgate Street. When Cornelius Elvin died in 1873, over 2,000 people attended his funeral.

As to local Roman Catholics, at the end of the 16th century recusants spent long periods in Bury Gaol, but the old faith survived and was advanced, mainly as a result of the work of the Jesuits. In 1633, the College of the Holy Apostles was founded, to provide for the needs of Catholics in the eastern counties and, after the Restoration, its headquarters were here. There was a chapel, visited by large numbers of townsfolk, in the Abbey Ruins, and the Superior of the College had a house there, while there was, somewhere in the town, a school for the children of Roman Catholics. The four years between 1684 and 1688 saw, for the only time before the 19th century, Roman Catholics serving as Corporation members, alongside Protestant Non-conformists and Anglicans. Matters might have prospered for longer had progress not been so rapid; 1688 saw a riot in the town in which Jesuits and their property were attacked, but mass was said in country houses round about at Hengrave, Lawshall and Coldham Hall and this helped to keep the faith alive. In the middle years of the 18th century, Fr John Gage, the younger brother of Sir Thomas Rookwood Gage of Hengrave, said mass in secret in the large house on the north corner of Southgate Street and St Botolph's Lane, until a property in Westgate Street was acquired in 1760, and a chapel built, dedicated to the Immaculate Conception on 20 December 1762. Worship seems to have been quite open, and it was formally licensed for public worship, under the 1789 Act, in 1791. The present Catholic Church, which was dedicated to St Edmund on 14 December 1837, was designed in the Jesuit style by Day of Worcester and in 1979, the Blessed Sacrament Chapel, the very Chapel built by Fr Gage in 1762, was brought back into use after forming part of the Presbytery for many years.

Higham's engraving of St Mary's, 1818, is accurate, showing both the south porch, the turret for the clock bell and the adjacent cottages as well as a wall around the garden on the south side of St Mary's. The Norman Tower is also shown with cupola and projecting dial. (JK)

ABOVE LEFT: John Nottyngham, an Abbeygate Street grocer, who died in 1439, left money to build a north and a west porch. If the west porch was ever built, no trace now remains, but the north porch is still a feature of the Church, though needing conservation. A pendant in the ceiling depicts God surrounded by angels. (JK)
RIGHT: The central panel on John Baret's tomb shows a figure holding a scroll with the word 'me' and wearing a collar of SS, awarded by Henry VI; it must be a portrait of this man whose chantry, though much mutilated, is still one of the finest features of the Church. BELOW LEFT: The decoration of the panels of the Baret chapel ceiling. Looking glass above it gives a star-like effect. RIGHT: Henry Le Keux's engraving of Mackenzie's drawing, published in 1849, shows the Church with north and south galleries, a western organ gallery, pulpit, and reading desk mid-way down the nave. The Mayor's pew is on the north, next the chancel arch. (JK)

48

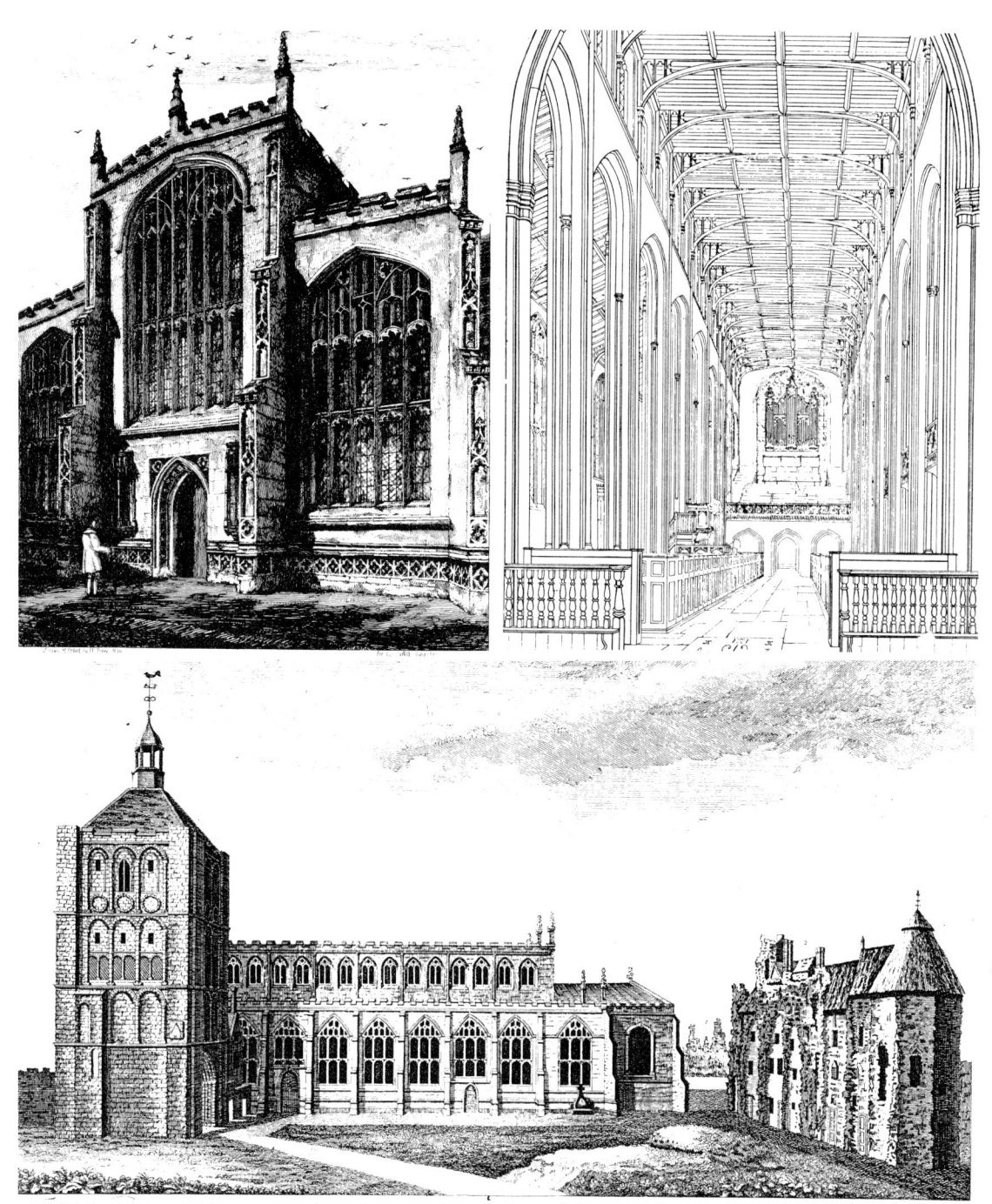

LEFT: Architectural features, such as the pear-shaped ogees of the tower butresses and the tracery of the west window, point to John Wastell, master mason at the Abbey, as the architect of the nave of St James's. Engraved by Davy, 1820. (JK) RIGHT: The nave of St James's Church, looking west, drawn by a member of the Lathbury family between 1827 and 1863-1864, when the new roof was erected. Note the organ, with the cherub on top at the west end, the pulpit about half way down the nave. The indent of the bell-founder's brass which is shown here in the foreground, is now under the Norman Tower. (SRO(B)) BELOW: Kirby's engraving of St James's Church, 1748, shows how it looked more like a Wastell building, before it was given a high-pitched roof. (St E)

ABOVE: The classical chancel was replaced by one of gothic style, designed by Sir Gilbert Scott in 1869.
LEFT: The interior of St James's Church c1917, showing the Victorian ceramic mosaics in the chancel. (BJH)
RIGHT: This sedan chair with wheels, now in Moyses Hall, is to be seen in several photographs dating from the 1890s, and is said to have been used to take ladies to St James's Church, perhaps for weddings. (SRO(B))

LEFT: In December 1913, St James's Church was designated the Cathedral church of the new Diocese of St Edmundsbury and Ipswich and, on 25 March 1914, the Right Reverend Henry Bernard Hodgson was enthroned as first Bishop of the new diocese. Here he knocks for admission to his cathedral. (RF) RIGHT: St John's Church, consecrated in 1841. (OGJ) BELOW: The Churchgate Street meeting house, built for the Presbyterian congregation in 1711; the building work was mainly carried out by members of the church. The roof was renewed a few years ago, but much more work is needed to ensure the future of this fine building.
(St E)

ABOVE: Many original fittings survive in Churchgate Street Chapel. Sadly, after the roof was repaired money was not available to replace the ceiling. (OGJ) BELOW: The Methodist Church in Brentgovel Street c1878. It replaced an earlier building in St Mary's Square which had become too small. (OGJ) OPPOSITE ABOVE: St Edmund's Roman Catholic Church was opened 150 years ago, a print of 1851. (JK) BELOW: St Peter's Church was built as a chapel-of-ease in St Mary's parish in 1858. (SRO(I))

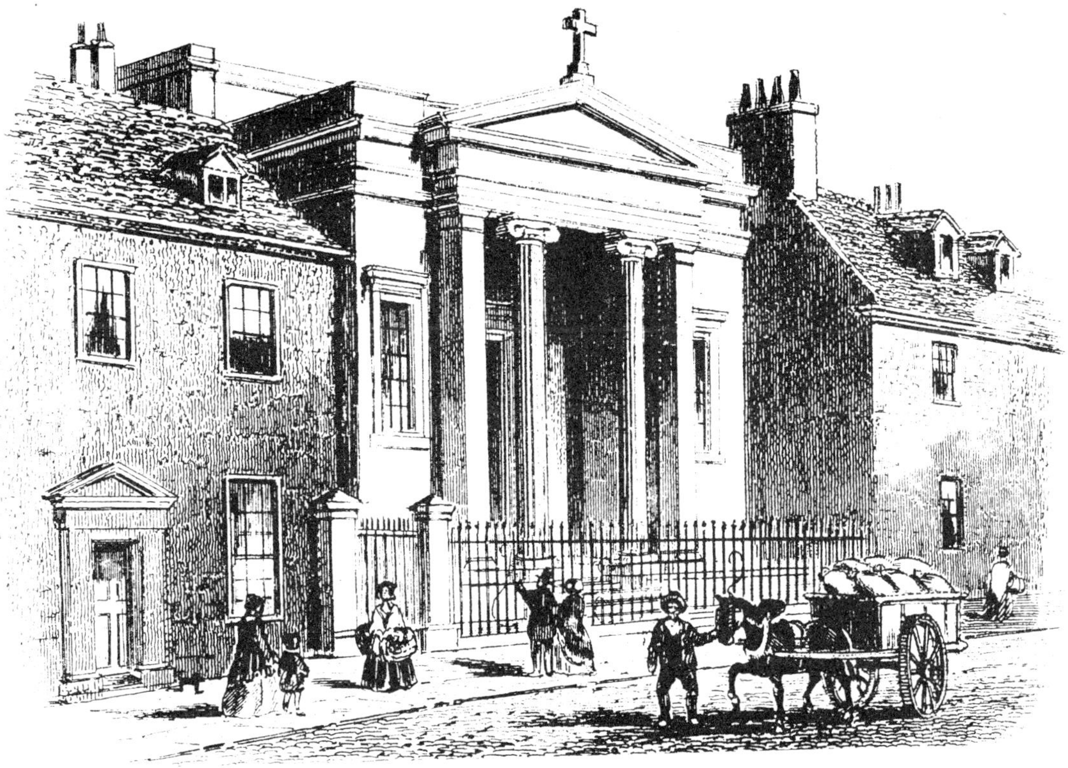

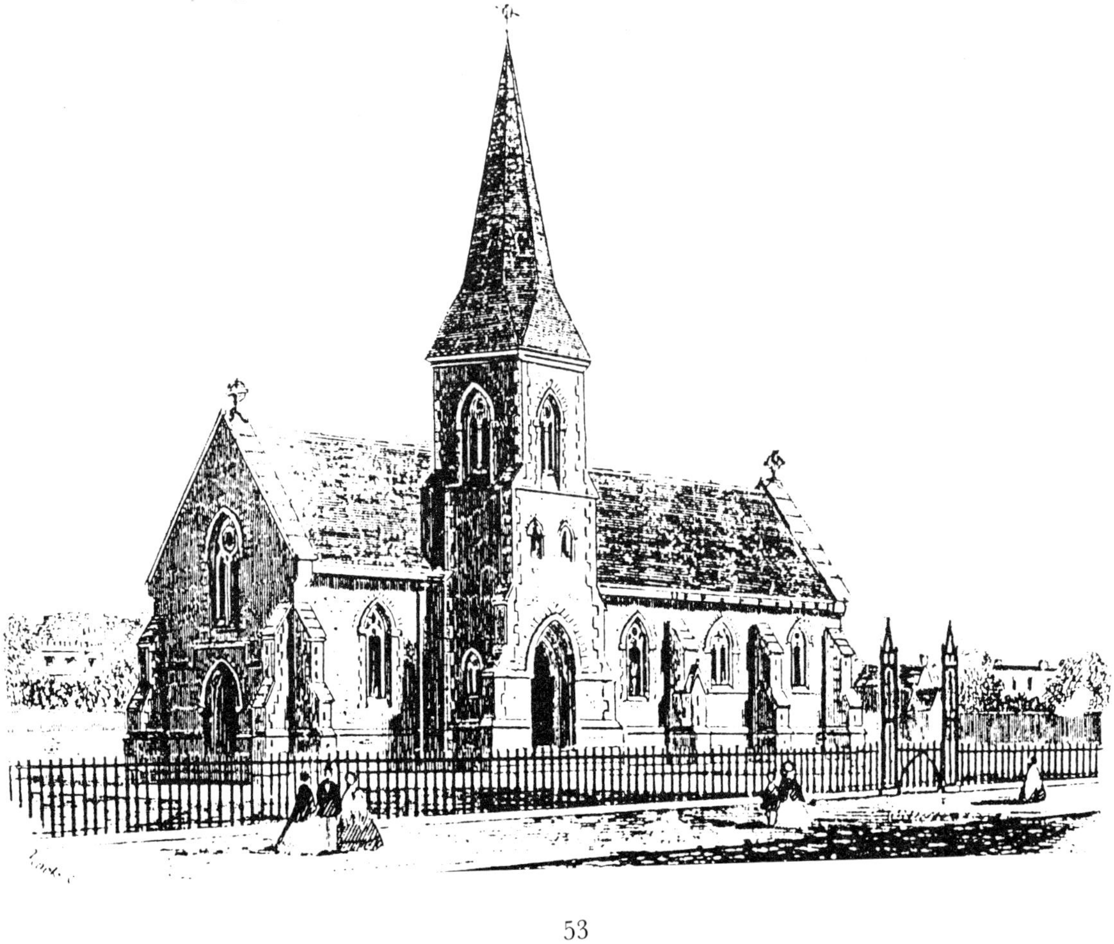

ABOVE: This brass, showing Jankyn Smyth, Bury's outstanding benefactor who died in 1481, and his wife Anne, is in St Mary's Church. Its heraldry, recorded by early antiquaries, provided clues which enabled information about his family to be discovered.(JK) BELOW: Every year a service is held to commemorate Jankyn Smyth and other benefactors of the town, at the conclusion of which shillings are presented to the residents of the Trust's almshouses. At the 500th anniversary service in 1981, Cllr Eric Steele, Mayor and one of the Trustees, presented the shillings. It is claimed to be the oldest endowed service in England.(OGJ)

Abbey and Borough

Two officers of the Abbey of St Edmund, the Cellarer and the Sacrist, had great influence within the town. The Cellarer had under his control a considerable quantity of agricultural land, mainly in the fields outside the town walls (for his principal function was to provide the food required to feed the monks), and at least five mills and three sheep folds. In the early days, all those who held land within the town, not just the Cellarer's own tenants, had been required to perform agricultural services, but by the time of Jocelin of Brakelond these had been commuted for money payments, which were already proving difficult to collect. *Rep Silver,* the payment made in lieu of reaping services, was one of these, and Jocelin tells how the townsmen built some stone houses in the market place, so that the rent they received could be used to pay it each year; the surviving accounts of the Sacrist regularly include an entry relating to this payment, which was initially made to him, and subsequently passed on to the Cellarer. The Cellarer also enjoyed the great privilege of buying the food he required for the community in the market at advantageous prices, while fishing in the Teyfen and in the river Lark above the Rothe (now Southgate) Bridge was his too. He also controlled the use made of the river by the washerwomen, and by the fullers who washed their cloth in it. As late as the time of Abbot Samson, the Cellarer's tenants were still subject to the jurisdiction of his courts, but they maintained archaic customs and, after one of his tenants, Ketel, was tried there for robbery, lost the judicial duel and was hung, there were demands that all those who lived in the town should be subject to the same jurisdiction. Had Ketel lived within the walls, he would have been tried by the oath of his neighbours and acquitted, so an agreement was made that such men should have burghal privileges and be tried in the Portmanmoot, while the Cellarer's court, held at his grange at Eastgate Barns, confined its activities to agricultural matters.

The Sacrist's influence in mediaeval Bury St Edmunds was all-pervading. His interest in the town is set out in a bull of Pope Eugenius III, who reigned from 1145-1154, which confirmed that the Borough of St Edmund had been assigned for the service of the Church and for the support of the office of Sacrist. The Sacrist collected many of the ancient and — later — much hated customary rents, which had to be paid by those living within the town, such as *landmol* and *hadgovel.* According to the tradition of the Abbey, which may not be entirely reliable, *landmol* was the sum of 2d paid for each of the 900 acres within the four crosses which belonged to Bederic (from whom *Bedricesworth* is said to have taken its name), while *hadgovel* was the traditional payment made for the original burgage tenements, and is first encountered during the time of Baldwin. Besides these, the Sacrist was one of, if not the, major property owner within the Borough and received rent from some 250 houses. He also controlled the courts and appointed and paid the bailiffs who sat in the Borough court, the Portmanmoot. Similarly, the Sacrist was responsible for the fairs and market, and took the toll paid by those who traded there. Burgesses who lived in *hadgovel* tenements were exempt from paying toll, and sometimes the Sacrist granted exemption to others, such as the Prior of Ixworth or the Friars of Babwell. Regulation of weights and measures and the enforcement of the assizes of bread and beer, which controlled the quality of these necessities, were also duties of the Sacrist, whose secular duties and sources of income in many ways foreshadow those of the Corporation after 1606.

At first, the townsmen were granted reasonably generous privileges, but these were not augmented as the town prospered. A guild merchant was established in the 12th century, perhaps as early as the time of Abbot Anselm, 1121-48, and by about 1200, the alderman of the guild merchant came to be identified with the alderman of the town. Had it not been for the reactionary attitude of the Abbey, the guild merchant in Bury St Edmunds would no doubt have developed until the town acquired borough status and it became the Corporation. Incorporation became the ambition of the townsmen and, from time to time, the tension between Abbey and town became such that the two parties resorted to litigation or even violence. There were many questions at issue in these disputes, both political and economic, such as the demand freely to elect the alderman and to appoint the keepers of the north, south, west and Risby gates (the Abbot always kept the east gate, which was close to the Abbey, in his own hand). Whether or not the townsmen had the right to have a guild merchant was also a frequent question and, from 1381 onwards, the customary payment of 100 marks (£66 13s 4d) to each new abbot on his election in lieu of homage became a constant source of friction.

Mediaeval Bury St Edmunds was so prone to rioting that it has recently been dubbed the Brixton of the 14th century. Perhaps the best known of these disputes is that which erupted in 1327, when the town was in a lawless state for the best part of two years. Charters and jewels were stolen by townsmen, some of the monks were imprisoned for a time in the Guildhall, and the Abbot was kidnapped and taken to Brabant. At one point townsmen besieged the precinct from a Sunday to the following Thursday, and, on several occasions, damage was done to buildings within the precinct; the Norman gateway into the court of the Abbey was destroyed or so badly damaged that it had to be replaced with the gateway we know as the Abbey Gate, which is said (although no evidence for this has been found), to have been built with the money which the town paid as a fine for their part in the rioting. A receipt for 50 marks, given by Abbot John of Barnham to Richard of Drayton and Ralph the butcher and others and dated 29 September 1349, which has survived among the Borough archives, marks the payment of the final instalment of the fine imposed in 1329.

At the height of the rising, the townsmen extorted from the Abbot what amounted to a charter of incorporation but, as soon as order was restored, this document was deemed null and void because it had been obtained under duress. One of the penalties imposed upon the town was that it lost the right even to hold the guild merchant. About then, however, the guild of the Purification of Our Lady in St James's Church (Candlemas Guild), was established, and there is little doubt that this was a re-creation of the guild merchant in an ostensibly religious form which, nevertheless, afforded its members an opportunity to meet to discuss matters of general concern to the town. In the 15th century, any one who had any position at all in the town belonged to this guild.

In time it became increasingly obvious that incorporation was unlikely to be obtained as long as the Abbey continued at the centre of affairs. Some of the townsmen's problems were solved by the establishment of the charity which is now known as the Guildhall Feoffment Trust. The statutes of Candlemas Guild were altered in 1472 to enable it to administer bequests to the town which had been made by two of its members, John, commonly called Jankyn, Smyth and Margaret Odeham. Jankyn Smyth, who died on 28 June 1481, left 238 acres of land in Bury St Edmunds and the surrounding villages to provide a fund from which the customary payment of a hundred marks, (payable, as explained above, on the election of each new abbot) could be met. When Margaret Odeham died in 1492, her principal beneficiaries were the prisoners in the gaol. Thomas Bereve also left legacies to the guild for the King's tax, the relief of prisoners and the upkeep of the Guildhall. Bury people have been adding to the endowments of this body ever since.

There is abundant evidence from 1570 onwards to show that the Feoffees had taken upon themselves many of the duties which would have fallen upon a corporation, had there been one in Bury St Edmunds; they were, for instance, already repairing the town gates and bridges and providing such things as the pillory, as well as enforcing the Elizabethan legislation designed to cope with the ever-increasing problem of poverty. It was probably the desire to obtain a grant from the Crown of the fairs, markets, tithes and the Almoner's Barns estate which made incorporation a necessity. The memoranda book of Thomas Bright the younger, who took the lead in obtaining the charter of incorporation, still survives among the archives of the Guildhall Feoffees. It contains the names of those who met at his house and agreed between them that they would meet the cost of incorporation, and also a subscription list of those who contributed towards the cost. A copy of the petition survives; it is undated, but must have been made before August 1601, when Sir Robert Jermyn wrote to Sir Robert Cecil to set out his objections to an incorporation for Bury St Edmunds.

The charter of 1606, (always so-called although technically the document should be described as Letters Patent) set up a corporation consisting of 37 members: the Alderman, very roughly equivalent to the Mayor nowadays, 12 Capital Burgesses and 24 Burgesses of the Common Council. Each year the Corporation was to elect four Assistants who were to be Justices of the Peace for the Borough, and the offices of Town Clerk and Recorder were established. The names of all the first office-holders are set out in the charter.

Any sense of achievement felt when the first charter was issued in April 1606 must have been tinged with regret that so much that had been asked for had not been granted, and the fragmentary accounts which have survived from this period show that further petitions were made as soon as the first grant had been received. Two years later, after a large part of the town had been seriously damaged by a fire, James I made a further grant to Bury St Edmunds. This (after confirming a gift of more than 500 loads of timber from Hitcham wood towards rebuilding) granted the reversion of a lease of the tithes, fairs and markets, which Thomas Bright and his associates were anxious to acquire to provide income to pay the stipends of the ministers and preachers of the two parish churches, thus enabling them to control the pulpits of the parish churches. These had been leased to Sir Robert Drury of Hawstead for 40 years in 1604, so the Corporation would derive no benefit from them until Sir Robert's lease expired in 1644. The Corporation were also granted a number of public buildings such as the Market Cross, the Tollhouse and the Gaol; these had all been destroyed or badly damaged in the fire, and the Corporation was made responsible for rebuilding them.

The Members of the Corporation had no intention of waiting nearly 40 years before they could enjoy these things, and in 1609 some of them, called the purchasers, bought in the reversion of Sir Robert Drury's lease. Large sums of money were needed for the charters and rebuilding the public buildings, while a sum in excess of £2,000 had to be found for the purchase of the lease. The 1608 charter alone cost over £300. Thomas Bright the elder, father of the Thomas who took the lead in obtaining the charters, had left £300 when he died in 1587 — as much as he left to any of his children — to the Guildhall Feoffees for the repair of the churches and clothing the poor. This money had never been invested in land, and the Feoffees managed to convince the Commissioners for Charitable Uses that so much benefit would be derived from the grant of 1608, that no better use could be found for Bright's gift. It must be said that, although this capital sum was put towards the cost of the charter, the annual payments for repairing the churches and clothing the poor were always made. Repayments were still being made to the Governors of the Grammar School for a loan in the 1650s, and it is probable that the loan from the Guildhall Feoffees was never repaid. Although the purchasers' surviving accounts show that they soon assumed responsibility for repairing the churches, sometimes with the aid of a church rate, it is also apparent that the Feoffees were still paying the town clergy as late as 1623.

The final grant from James 1 was made in 1614, and it gave the town important privileges, including the right to return two members to Parliament, to hold a separate court of quarter sessions for the Borough, and to have its own Coroner (an office always held by the immediate past Alderman). Bury St Edmunds can also be added to the City of London and 16 provincial corporations, noted by Professor Christopher Hill in his *Economic Problems of the Church*, which exercised ecclesiastical patronage.

After all the effort that had been expended to acquire, at last, borough status for Bury St Edmunds, it is almost incredible to find that, in 1630, the corporate estates were conveyed to a body of feoffees. One source suggests that it was considered that some things could be better managed by men in their individual capacities, rather than as a body corporate, while another stated that it was feared that the charter might be withdrawn; no reason is suggested, but it could be the result of the Corporation's radical attitude towards its ecclesiastical patronage. Greater public participation was another reason given but, on the face of it, this does not seem plausible, for the 40 feoffees of the corporate lands were the 37 corporation members plus the Town Clerk, Recorder and one other. Whether this arrangement initially made much difference cannot be determined, as the minute books of the Corporation are missing until 1652 but, from then until the Restoration, it looks as though there was little, if any, practical difference. This was not the case at the Restoration.

During the Commonwealth, the Bury St Edmunds Corporation was firmly behind Parliament and, at the Restoration of Charles II, 19 of the 37 members refused to renounce the Solemn League and Covenant. The Restoration Commissioners then removed these members from the Corporation and replaced them with men who were sympathetic to the King but, as a result of the feoffment, those members who had been deposed still had, with their former colleagues, a legal title to the corporate estates. It was only in 1668, after a lengthy suit in Chancery, that the Corporation was granted another charter, which confirmed their title to the corporate estates, and the 'pretended feoffees', as they were sometimes called, were compelled to reconvey the estates to the then Alderman and Burgesses. In the meantime, the Corporation had had to fulfil its responsibilities for, to take but one example, paying the stipends of the town clergy, while the 'pretended feoffees' had been receiving the rents from the corporate estates.

From 1684 until 1688 the Corporation was governed by a new charter of Charles II, which gave the Crown the right to nominate members. Although there were the same number of members, they were now known as the Mayor, Alderman and Burgesses of Bury St Edmunds, and this charter gave Bury St Edmunds the right to have a sword of state carried before the Mayor on formal occasions. Because the Crown could nominate and remove members of the Corporation at will, Charles II was able to pack it with men who supported his religious policy. For the first and only time before the 19th century, the town's governing body included people who represented all shades of religious opinion, from Roman Catholics to Non-conformists.

The Justices of the Peace, the Corporation and the parish officers all had their respective responsibilities for poor relief and highways. In 1747, the two Bury St Edmunds parishes were incorporated for poor law purposes, and a court of Guardians of the Poor was set up, consisting of the Alderman, Recorder, Coroner, Assistant Justices and Capital Burgesses of the Borough, as well as six inhabitants of each parish. Although the Court of Guardians had been granted certain powers for the general improvement of the town, it was really only in 1811, when an Act of Parliament was obtained to establish Improvement Commissioners for the town, that real advances were made. Even technical matters such as road building here, as elsewhere, had been in the hands of amateurs, often reluctant to take office, until James McAdam was appointed the Commissioners' surveyor in 1821.

Local government as we know it really began with the Municipal Corporation Act of 1835. This replaced the old, self-perpetuating oligarchy with an elected council. Only one member of the old

Corporation, George Creed, a surgeon, was prepared to admit that some measure of reform was required. The governing body then consisted of a Mayor, Recorder, six Aldermen and 18 Councillors and, for the first time, elections were held to choose representatives for the three wards into which the town was then divided. The handover from the old Corporation to the Town Council was not without problems, for the old body was greatly in debt, and Abraham Gall, the last Alderman, refused to hand over the insignia and plate and even, it seems, intended to sell it in an endeavour to reduce the corporate debt, but the new Council succeeded in obtaining a judgement that it was to be handed over to them.

After the Commemoration Service, the 'Cakes and Ale' ceremony is held in the Guildhall. This photograph of c1960 shows Mr Bevis Southgate proposing the traditional toast to the memory of Jankyn Smyth, the founder of the Guildhall Feoffment Trust. Also in the photograph are Canon Pelly, Cllr and Mrs Aubrey Wilkes, Mrs Dorothy Bright and Miss Hardwick. (SRO(B))

ABOVE LEFT: Stephen Gardiner, Bishop of Winchester and Lord Chancellor under Mary, and the son of a Bury clothmaker, retained links with the town throughout his life. Like the Lord Keeper, he may have helped to minimise the impact of the dissolution of the guilds on the Feoffees.(SRO(B)) RIGHT: Lord Keeper Bacon, who had many interests in the town and was one of the Feoffees, served his term as Alderman (albeit by deputy) in 1573. In 1562 he wrote to the Feoffees, refusing to help them get a charter, since too many corporations had been granted then.(SRO(B)) BELOW LEFT: Some of the considerable cost of obtaining the charter of incorporation was met by a public subscription; Thomas Bright's memoranda book notes those townspeople who subscribed £68 5s 0d.(SRO(B)) RIGHT: The oldest part of the Guildhall is the inner entrance arch of c1250, from the porch (remodelled in the 15th century) to the hall itself.(RCHM)

ABOVE: The tercentenary of the granting of the charter was celebrated on 3 April 1906, when it was read from the steps of the Angel. (OGJ) BELOW: Above the comparatively modern Guildhall ceilings is a fifteenth century roof with both king and queen posts on each tie beam. In the foreground is the elaborate scissor truss at the dais end, while beyond can be seen the normal type of truss. (RCHM)

ABOVE LEFT: The Guildhall porch was remodelled after Jankyn Smyth died, to provide the safe place he demanded for keeping the money from his bequest, and for deeds and other documents concerning the land. Well into this century there were verses extolling Jankyn Smyth on the wall in the Evidence House (the room above the porch), above the wall safe in which valuables were kept. Some of the town records were kept in the Evidence House until the Muniment Room opened in 1938. (JK) RIGHT: Alderman John Ridley Hooper, Mayor of Bury St Edmunds, 1910-1911 and 1920-1921, in the court room of the Guildhall. He is wearing the Mayor's robe and chain, the gift of James Oakes in 1805, while the maces are held in special brackets either side of the portrait of King James I and the sword of state rests on the table before him.(OGJ) BELOW LEFT: George Creed's protest against the Corporation's petition against the Municipal Corporation Act, 1835.(SRO(B)) RIGHT: Francis King Eagle, first Mayor after the Municipal Corporation Act, 1835, was the 1832 radical candidate following the Reform Act. An eminent tithe lawyer, he became County Court Judge in 1846 and, on his death in 1854, a monument to him was erected by public subscription.(OGJ)

ABOVE: East Gate Bridge before it was rebuilt in 1840.(JK) BELOW: St Botolph's Bridge, Raingate Street, in 1848. (SRO(B))

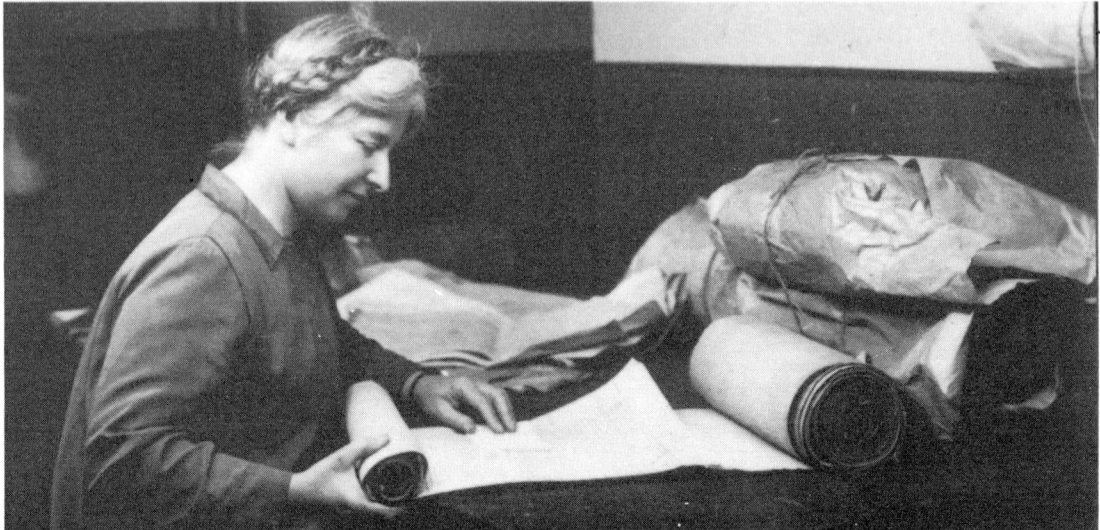

ABOVE: Mediaeval work was discovered in the bridge under Southgate Street on 2nd August, 1970. Dr Stanley West and Geoffrey Moss are shown examining the structure (SRO(B)) BELOW: Without the Archives of the Corporation and the Guildhall Feoffees, it would be impossible to study the history of Bury St Edmunds. Miss L. J. Redstone was appointed Archivist when the Muniment Room in the Borough Offices opened in 1938. This developed into the Bury St Edmunds branch of the Suffolk Record Office.

Those in Need

Bury's 16th century benefactor, Thomas Bereve, set up some almshouses in Burmans (now Pump) Lane which, after the reformation, were run by the Guildhall Feoffees. Bereve wanted his almshouses, which stood on part of the site of the Garland Street Baptist Church, to remain as such for ever, so he assigned two shillings out of the rent of two adjacent tenements, which he had let by lease, towards their upkeep. He left these leases to his wife, Joan, for her life, and after her death to the priest who served at the altar of St Thomas à Becket in St James's Church, who was to spend the income on the almshouses and 'have Thomas Bereve in remembrance every day'.

On 8 December 1582, the Guildhall Feoffees made orders for their almshouses: those who were appointed to them had to promise, before the Feoffees assembled in the Guildhall, 'that he or she shall lyve in peace and quietnes without braweling, dronkenes, ydlenes . . . and kepe them selves in some profitable and comendable occupacion or exercise to the best of their power and knowledge And that they shalbe redy at all tymes to kepe such persones as shalbe sicke within this towne of Bury and attende diligently upon them . . . And that they shall willingly receive and suffer to contynue with them in the almose house to them appointed any one person hereafter at any tyme to be assigned unto them . . . And for defalt of performynge of the promises aforesaid they shalbe removed and put out of the said almoise houses as persones unworthie to receive suche almoise'. The almshouse concept has changed considerably over the centuries.

A different arrangement was envisaged by Dr Poley Clopton when he set up Clopton's Hospital or asylum. He provided accommodation for six poor widows and six poor widowers, three of each from each parish, who were over sixty years of age and who had lived in the town for a year and a day. These were people who had paid all their rates and taxes and had received no parochial relief — the term 'decayed trades people' was used to describe them in Victorian times. In 1735, the Trustees bought a site in the churchyard, on which they built a handsome building, now the Provost's House, at a cost of £1,894 0s 2d (including the site), plus a hundred guineas for legal costs. The first residents were elected on 8 September 1744 and their trades were noted—two tailors, a butcher, a gardener, a peruke maker and a glover. One who ended his days in Clopton's Hospital was Ralph Guest, who died in 1830. He had been the organist at St Mary's and taught music in the town. His will conjures a picture of his room, with its treasured music, books, prints, china and silver, much of which he left to friends who had visited him in the hospital. Dr Clopton's trustees sold the house in 1898, since when the greater part has been used as the home of the Vicar of St James's who, since 1914, has been Provost of the Cathedral.

The Fennell Homes, often called the Quaker Cottages, in St Andrews Street, must be among the oldest purpose-built flats in Bury St Edmunds. The Fennells were a well-to-do Quaker brother and sister who lived at 2, St Mary's Square, and were reputedly reluctant to pay their contributions to the Friends' funds. After their deaths, their money was inherited by a Mrs Hare, who used it to found the homes. They were originally intended for Quaker women with a little income of their own who, in return for their accommodation, were willing to do whatever they could to promote the work of the Friends.

Homelessness is no new problem; the community has often had to make provision for housing those who are unable to house themselves. A workhouse, the last refuge for those who, though prepared to work, were for one reason or another unable to support themselves, was established in a house in Whiting Street before 1621. Then in the spring of 1622, a house in Churchgate Street, given to the Feoffees by Richard Walker, the first Alderman of Bury St Edmunds, was adapted for this purpose. By 1630 (probably in 1626) the Feoffees had bought Moyses Hall, which afforded room for the town gaol and the house of correction, as well as the workhouse. The workhouse was removed from Moyses Hall before the two parishes were incorporated for poor law purposes in 1747 for, at that time, there was a workhouse for St James's parish in Eastgate Street, and one for St Mary's parish in Schoolhall Street.

A list of College Street Workhouse inmates in 1765 shows that there were then 30 men between the ages of 22 and 84, including the octogenarian John Kenyon who kept the gate; 53 women aged between 20 and 85, and 28 boys and 38 girls up to 18 years of age—a total of 149. Of these, three men and seven women suffered some form of mental illness. This building continued to be used after the adoption of the Poor Law Amendment Act of 1834 until 1884, when the inmates were removed to the Thingoe Union Workhouse, which is now St Mary's Day Hospital. Many of the workhouse buildings in College Street were demolished then, but some of those retained were used by the St Edmunds Working Men's Association which provided, among other things, a reading room and a ragged school. One of the buildings was used as the Scout Headquarters until the early 1960s.

The house of correction was intended to reform sturdy beggars and incorrigible rogues, and the Feoffees established one for the whole town in 1580, replacing earlier houses of correction for the two parishes. This was in Master Andrewes Street which, because a bridewell is another name for a house of correction, is now called Bridewell Lane. In 1589, the county magistrates made an agreement with the Feoffees, whereby the house of correction in Bridewell Lane for a time served both the town and the Liberty of St Edmund. The rules for running the house of correction illustrate the harsh life imposed upon those taken there. It was under the general supervision of four wardens, two of whom had to live in Bury St Edmunds, while the other two were, if possible, to be selected from among the chief constables of the Liberty. On admission to the house, inmates were chained and whipped, while more severe punishment might be inflicted on those whose subsequent conduct was unsatisfactory. By four o'clock in the morning in summer and five in the winter, they had to be up, dressed and ready for work. The day began (and ended) with a set form of prayers in the hall, and continued until seven in the evening, with a break only for dinner and supper. On days when meat was eaten, the inmates were given for each meal eight ounces of rye bread, a pint of porridge, a quarter of a pound of meat and a pint of beer of the (very strong) rate of three combes of barley, to a barrel containing 36 gallons. The diet for fish days is difficult to understand, but it seems that on those days the porridge was to be made with milk or peas and that, instead of meat, they were given either a third of a pound of cheese or one good herring or 'two white or redd' (salt and smoked?). A little extra bread and beer might be given to those who worked well, at the discretion of the keeper. If possible, the house of correction was to be maintained by voluntary contributions, but if this could not be done, a rate had to be made. The Guildhall Feoffees used a rent charge of £40 a year out of the manor of Torksey in Lincolnshire, which had been left to them in 1573 by Sir Edmund Jermyn, to pay for the house.

In earlier centuries, relief to the poor was more likely by way of occasional gifts of food, fuel, clothing or money and, once again, Thomas Bereve's will gives an idea of what might be expected. 200 bundles of wood were to be given to poor people each year for seven years at Christmas, and the same amount at Candlemas (2 February), or earlier if his executors should think fit. For five years after his death, 12 shirts and smocks, and for seven years a cade (a barrel containing five or six hundred) of herrings were to be distributed. The poor were also to be given £3 6s 8d within a week of his burial and the same amount after the ceremonies which marked the thirtieth day after his burial. In addition, for seven years after his death, a further sum of 3s 4d was to be given on All Saints Day and on Good Friday.

Eventually many charities were endowed, which enabled the Feoffees to provide necessities for the poor each year. Some benefactors, such as Thomas Bright the elder, who died in 1587, left money for clothing for a large number of poor people; others, like Peter Kembold, the first part of whose legacy was received in 1604, left money to relieve the poor in certain parts of the town, in his case, the north and east wards.

At the end of the 16th century and beginning of the 17th, Bury St Edmunds had to face many social and economic problems. The cloth-making industry, on which the town's prosperity had long depended, was in decline, while a rising birth rate was aggravated by constant immigration, usually from near-by villages, but sometimes farther afield. A large proportion of the working population must have always been on or near to the poverty line and a bad harvest, causing prices to rise, could easily create a crisis.

At times of exceptional hardship, extraordinary relief had to be given, and every effort was always made to provide work to enable the poor to keep themselves. In 1594, one of the years when prices were high, the Feoffees set aside £80 0s 0d for a stock with which to provide materials to set the poor to work; the money would have been used to buy wool, to be carded and spun, if not woven and finished. It was also in that year that Overseers of the Poor first appeared in Bury St Edmunds but, instead of being appointed for the two parishes, they were appointed for the five wards, seven for the east and six for each of the others; what 31 overseers did is not explained. Fuel was also dear, and in May the Feoffees allocated £60 0s 0d to buy coal from Lynn, which was stored in a yard between St James's Church and the Norman Tower, where two men attended two days a week to deliver it to the eligible poor.

Another time of great hardship followed the failure of the 1622 harvest. All the corn received as rent, as well as four additional combes bought by the Feoffees, was ground, baked and given to the poor, and unusually large sums of money were also distributed. When the harvest failed there was always trouble, because some growers contracted to supply buyers with their crops before harvest; these bargains were often strictly enforced and could lead to little grain coming into the market. Some effort to provide meal for the poor at prices they could afford is indicated by the 11s 5d paid for 'bord and workemanshipp for a bing (a bin) at the Market Crosse to putt in meale to serve the poore.' Another item relates to two shillings 'given to a scrivener for writing a lettre that was sent to the Lords of the Counsell for Certificat of their proceedinge touching the abatinge of the price of corne'. A copy of this letter survives among the State Papers Domestic, and shows that on 27 January 1623 the county magistrates had written to the Privy Council, seeking guidance about the implementation of a proclamation which forbade millers to buy and sell grain. It had been usual for millers in Bury St Edmunds to buy grain, grind it, and sell it to the poor in smaller quantities than they were able to buy it in the market. The letter for which the scrivener was paid two shillings is dated 29 January, and it is a report by the Alderman and Burgesses on the action they had taken following the proclamation. As the town was a great malting place, they had forbidden malting for three weeks, and afterwards, only allowed it once a week, in the hope that quantities of barley might be used for bread. Instead of this, however, barley had ceased to come into the market; twenty ale houses had been closed down, and the price of beer kept down to 7s 4d and 4s 0d the barrel. Malting had been forbidden by any but maltsters, and only lawful dealers were allowed to buy more corn than was required by their families for a week. Finally, they reported that they had ventured partially to tolerate the sale of meal by millers for fear of 'a mutiny among the poor'. It seems that Bury St Edmunds was close to, if not actually experiencing, famine conditions, and there was a possibility of rioting.

It was then that the workhouse was established in Churchgate Street; considerable sums of money were also spent that year on setting up St Peter's Hospital in Out Risbygate as a house of correction. When the earlier joint arrangement with the county magistrates ceased is not clear but, as no unusually large sums had been spent on the house since 1589, it is possible that the exceptional conditions had forced a change in arrangements which had otherwise worked well for quite a long time.

The harvest failed again in 1631 and, when it became obvious that the poor would not be able to afford corn, the authorities set up a scheme to provide it at reasonable prices. In accordance with instructions from the Crown, the Alderman and Burgesses had done what they could to restrain the ingrossers (who contracted to buy crops before harvest) and maltsters within their jurisdiction. A number of trustworthy men were sent into Norfolk, where there was plenty of corn, to buy an adequate supply and bring it to Bury St Edmunds. No one was taxed towards the cost of this, but 'maltsters and ingrossers of the towne that had bought forehand bargaines were ordered to bring some quanteties of corne in the market, yet at such prices as they gayned in every quarter of corne 4s 0d above what it cost them'. The better-off had voluntarily given £137 0s 0d, and others had lent, interest-free, sums amounting to £600. Forty men were employed in managing this stock for the relief of the poor during thirty weeks when prices were high. All the money borrowed was repaid, and only that which had been freely given was used to make up the loss.

Countless instances of local initiative designed to relieve hardship caused by lack of food or exceptionally severe weather can be found in later centuries. The young gentlemen of the Grammar School performed a play each year, and sometimes gave the profit to buy food and fuel for the poor. This was the case in 1784 when they put on *The Orphan of China* by Murphy and Coote in the Assembly Room; they gave the large sum of £40 0s 0d to be 'distributed amongst those whose distressed situation at this inclement season makes them the most deserving objects of our charity'. The following year an engraving was published, showing the boys offering the proceeds of their play to charity.

Medical care of some kind was provided by the Abbey, under whose auspices a number of hospitals were founded. Some of these seem to have been more like almshouses than a modern hospital, but care for lepers was provided at St Peter's Hospital in Out Risbygate, which was founded by Abbot Anselm, (1121—1148). Originally, St Petronilla's Hospital, which was also founded in the 12th century, and stood just outside the South Gate, afforded help to female lepers, but it seems to have been re-founded in the 15th century to serve the poor.

An early endowment was given to the Guildhall Feoffees by a priest, Sir John Frenze, to found a leper hospital at the corner of Risbygate Street and Chalk Road, which was sometimes called Spittle House Lane. It seems to have served as an isolation hospital on many occasions, until the pest houses were built in Sexton's Meadows in 1665. In the 19th century, when there was the threat of a cholera epidemic, it was suggested that the 'spittle house', as Frenze's Hospital was known, should be refurbished in case of need.

In the past, epidemics of virulent infectious diseases created greater problems than today. From its first appearance in 1348 until it virtually disappeared after 1666, plague was a great scourge. A Papal Bull survives in the Hertfordshire County Record Office which authorised the ordination at Bury St Edmunds of ten monks under the canonical age of 25, to replace those who had died in the Black Death. From then until the 17th century, plague was never far away, and from time to time broke out in an epidemic which might well wipe out a substantial proportion of the population. One expedient was to isolate those suffering from the plague by providing them with tents, as was done in Bury St Edmunds in 1589, when the Feoffees spent 5s 0d on tent poles—fortunately, plague was predominantly a disease of the summer months. On other occasions, whole families in which there had been a case of plague were boarded up in their houses until all danger of infection had passed, and there are several years in the early 17th century in which payments were made to the constables, who had to take food and other necessities to these unfortunate people.

A particularly serious outbreak occurred in 1637, when about 10% of the population died within some nine months. Those who could, generally the better off, escaped from the town to the country, where the infection was thought to spread less rapidly than in the densely populated, rat-infested town streets. Because so many families had to be confined to their houses, trade came to a standstill and contributions towards the relief of the people of Bury St Edmunds came from all over the county. A good idea of the devastation caused by the plague comes from the figures given in a church brief, an appeal for help read out in churches throughout the country, dated 17 November 1637. This stated that, although all the chief inhabitants and tradesmen had fled to the country, there were still 4,000 people who had not been infected, though 103 families were shut up in their houses and 117 people were sick of sores and under treatment. Already 439 people had been cured, but more than 600 died (it is obvious from the parish registers that, when things were at their worst, it had proved impossible to note the names of all those who had died); 263 families were infected. All of these had to be kept at the common expense, at more than £200 a week, and over £2,000 had already been disbursed.

During the plague epidemic of 1637, St Peter's pit in Out Risbygate was used as a communal burial place, while the former St Peter's Hospital, which seems to have been used for purposes akin to its original function several times in the late 16th and early 17th century, was used to accommodate those infected. It belonged to the governors of the Grammar School; their accounts for 1641—1642 reflect a certain amount of trouble there, as a payment of £20 0s 0d was made by Richard Gippes, receiver 'of the contribution mony for the late infection' to the Governors in respect of 'the detryment sustened by the burneinge of the houses of St Peters by the infected people there placed by the then Alderman in the tyme of the late visitation of the pestilence'.

In 1665, the year of the great plague in London, Bury St Edmunds fortunately remained free from infection, although the disease was rife in nearby villages. The Corporation had taken all possible precautions to ensure that infection did not enter the town, even forbidding one of their own number, Thomas Bull, landlord of the Angel and the common carrier, to take his waggons to London. The town gates were watched to see that no one entered the town, and pest houses, one of which still survives in Sextons Meadows, were built should they be needed.

Although the pest houses were, fortunately, never required to isolate plague victims, they were to be used frequently during epidemics of smallpox. From 1757 there is a register of all the inhabitants of St Mary's parish, which indicates those who had had smallpox naturally, those who had already been innoculated and those who had no protection against the disease whatsoever.

Before the establishment of a hospital in 1826, the Guildhall Feoffees had long provided some medical care for those unable to pay a doctor's fee. Their accounts record payments to surgeons from 1575, and from 1591 a surgeon called Lichfield was paid an annual retainer; later the surgeon retained by the Feoffees was called the Town Surgeon. An unusual item in the account for 1582 records a payment to a woman surgeon of Colchester.

A dispensary in Angel Lane, opposite the Angel yard, was the forerunner of the Suffolk General Hospital, the first hospital in the modern sense in Suffolk, which opened on 4 January 1826, in a building which had been constructed as an ordnance depôt during the Napoleonic wars. It was, of course, a voluntary hospital until 1948, when it was taken over by the National Health Service. Until then, a great deal of local effort was expended in raising the money needed to support it. The bazaars held in aid of the hospital, under the patronage of many prominent local families, were important events in the Victorian social calendar. These raised considerable sums and there were also many regular local subscribers, while the first scheme drawn up by the Charity Commissioners for the Guildhall Feoffment Trust assigned a proportion of the trust's income to the hospital.

ABOVE: St Peter's Hospital, Out Risbygate, by Isaac Johnson, 1754-1835.(SRO(I)) LEFT: Window tracery which used to form part of a rockery at St Peter's Cottage, Out Risbygate, which stands on the site of the hospital, c1955.(SRO(B)) RIGHT: A drawing, probably by Isaac Johnson, of St Nicholas Hospital, at the junction of Hollow Road and Barton Road, after the window from St Petronilla's had been moved there by Philip Bennet of Rougham. Undated, but probably early 19th century (JK)

ABOVE: Godfrey's print of St Petronilla's Hospital at Southgate Green was published in 1781, before the window was moved to St Nicholas' Hospital.(JK) BELOW: St Saviour's Hospital, founded by Abbot Samson before 1185-1187, was more an almshouse than a hospital in the modern sense.(JK)

ABOVE: The only view of Moyses Hall before the east wall fell in 1804 shows no cupola. It must date from before this, so the artist must have omitted it.(St E) BELOW: As a precaution to keep infection out of the town, and to prepare for a possible epidemic during the year of the Great Plague in London, pest houses were built in Great Sexton's Meadow. They were never used to isolate plague victims, but were used during other epidemics, especially of smallpox.(PPS)

Moyses Hall, originally a Norman merchant's house, then the Bridewell or magistrates' prison for many years, in an etching by Henry Davy published in 1827. (JK)

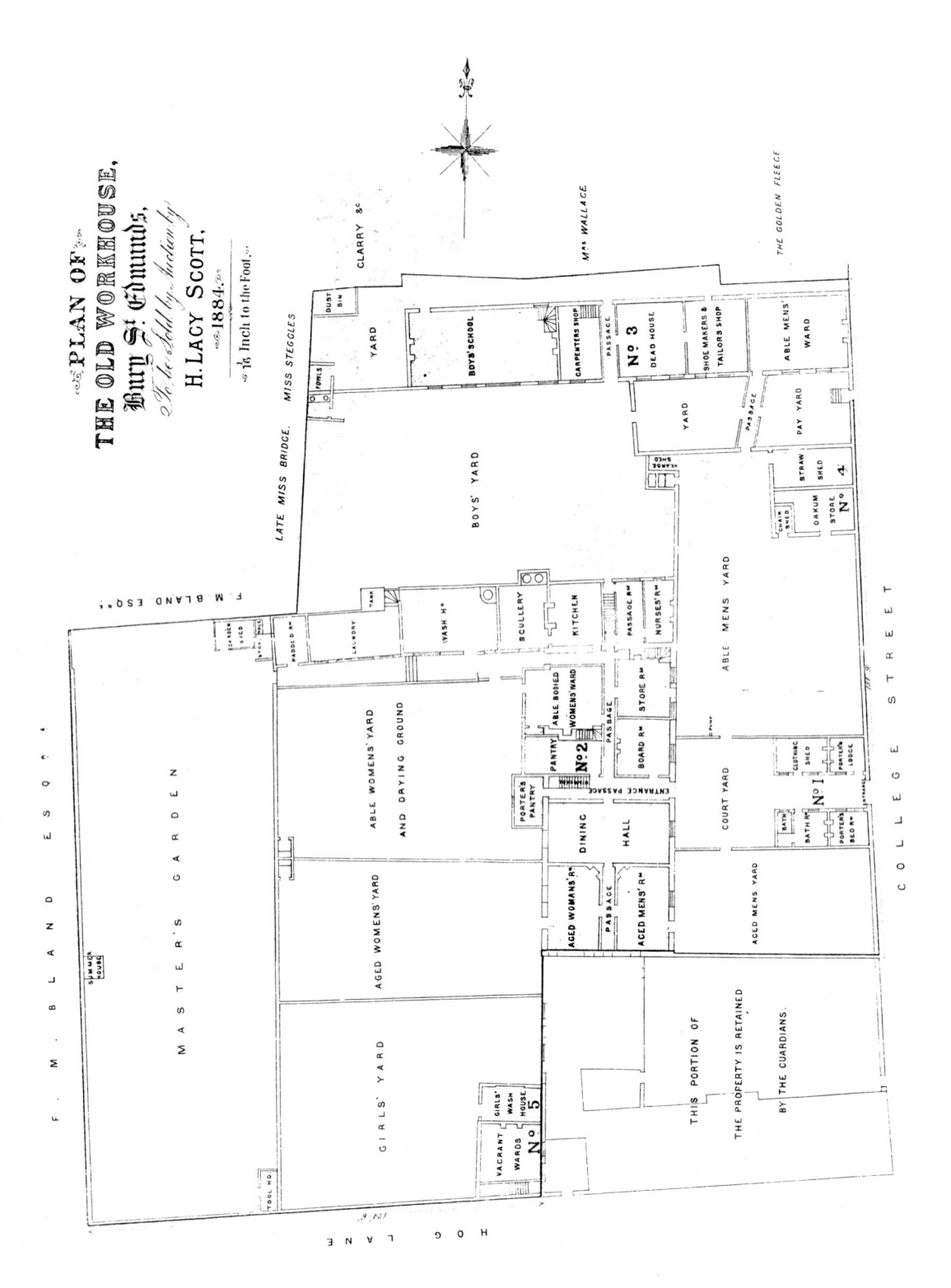

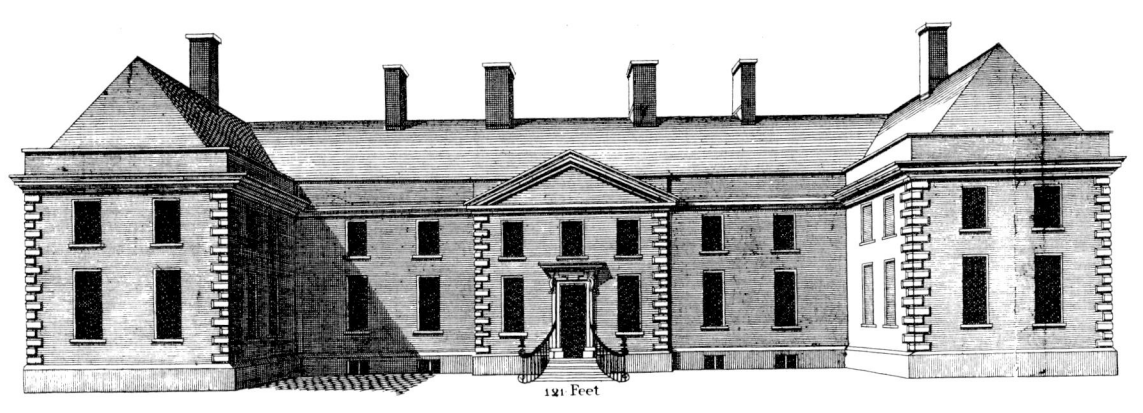

OPPOSITE: Plan of the workhouse from the sale particulars, 1884. (SRO(B)) ABOVE: Clopton's Hospital gave a home to respectable tradespeople of both sexes. BELOW: The College Street Workhouse when the inmates were removed to the Thingoe Union House in 1884. The central block is reputed to have been built on the site of the College of Jesus, which became a private house after the dissolution. Francis Pynner was once the owner and, immediately before it became the Workhouse, it was a girls' boarding school. (OGJ)

Angel Hill	Jo.ʰ Papavine	" 2 "	" 0 "	" 0 "	" 0 "	" 0 "
	Roger Prickle	" 10 "	" 2 "	" 1 "	" 0 "	" 1 "
	Mrs Burroughs	" 7 "	" 4 "	" 0 "	" 0 "	" 0 "
	M.ʳ Oldham	" 4 "	" 1 "	" 0 "	" 0 "	" 1 "
	Ed.ʷᵈ Evas	" 6 "	" 0 "	" 0 "	" 0 "	" 0 "
	Bennett	" 3 "	" 3 "	" 0 "	" 2 "	" 1 "
	Bob.ᵗ Candler	" 4 "	" 2 "	" 0 "	" 2 "	" 0 "
	Philip Winterflood S.ʳ	" 8 "	" 0 "	" 1 "	" 0 "	" 2 "
	Bryan Hill	" 4 "	" 0 "	" 0 "	" 0 "	" 0 "
	Burroughs Sharp	" 4 "	" 0 "	" 0 "	" 0 "	" 0 "
	Geo. Semple	" 7 "	" 1 "	" 0 "	" 0 "	" 1 "
	Wid.ʷ Black	" 3 "	" 1 "	" 0 "	" 0 "	" 0 "
	W.ᵐ Whiting	" 2 "	" 0 "	" 0 "	" 0 "	" 0 "
Philip Mazurier 2.ᵈ	Wid.ʷ Roots	" 5 "	" 0 "	" 1 "	" 0 "	" 0 "
Chequer Square	Phil. Mazurier	" 12 "	" 0 "	" 1 "	" 0 "	" 2 "
	M.ʳ Wood	" 3 "	" 1 "	" 0 "	" 1 "	" 0 "
	Mrs Ray	" 3 "	" 0 "	" 2 "	" 0 "	" 0 "
	Miss Ewing	" 5 "	" 2 "	" 0 "	" 0 "	" 0 "
Crown Street	Eliz Mendham	" 3 "	" 0 "	" 0 "	" 0 "	" 3 "
	John Mitchell	" 3 "	" 0 "	" 0 "	" 0 "	" 0 "
	Wid.ʷ Prick	" 2 "	" 0 "	" 0 "	" 0 "	" 0 "
	Wid.ʷ Clark	" 3 "	" 0 "	" 0 "	" 0 "	" 1 "
	Wid.ʷ Welch	" 3 "	" 0 "	" 1 "	" 0 "	" 0 "
	W.ᵐ Hale	" 2 "	" 0 "	" 0 "	" 0 "	" 0 "

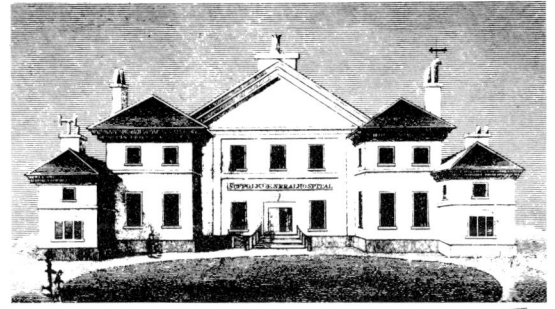

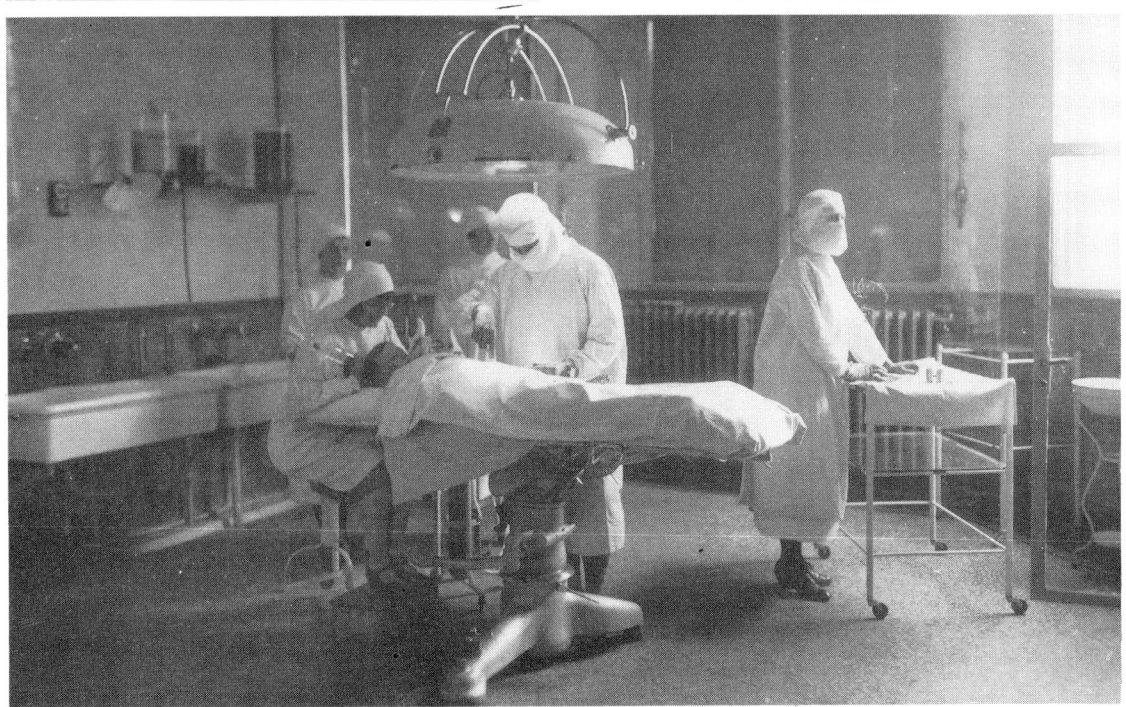

OPPOSITE ABOVE: Inhabitants of Angel Hill and Chequer Square, from the 1757 smallpox register for St Mary's parish.(SRO(B)) BELOW: The Suffolk General Hospital about 1830.(JK) LEFT: The Hospital's first building was originally an ordnance depôt for 10,000 stand of arms, built during the Napoleonic Wars.(JK) RIGHT: The Hospital in 1851 proclaimed in large letters that it was supported by voluntary contributions.(JK) CENTRE: An operating theatre during the 1930s. It is believed that the 'surgeon' was Dr H.M. Bird and that the 'anaesthetist' was Dr E.J. Cockram.(OGJ) BELOW: The Hospital in 1945.(OGJ)

ABOVE: Bury St Edmunds Corporation steam roller, an Aveling Porter 10-ton compound roller bought in 1911. Driver thought to be a Mr Kerry.(SRO(B)) BELOW: The town fire brigade c1906.(OGJ)

Rules and Regulations

Originally responsibility for roads and streets had rested with landowners, and money was often left to augment their efforts; Thomas Bereve, for instance, left 13s 4d for repairing Burmans Lane where he lived, and nearby Garland Street. The Highway Act of 1555 placed responsibility for mending roads on the unpaid parish highway surveyor, and the scanty records suggest that attention was piecemeal. In Bury St Edmunds things got better only when the Improvement Commissioners appointed James McAdam to be their Surveyor in 1821, following a scathing report on the state of the roads and means that had been taken to repair them. In that report he commented that materials were bought improperly and that expensive ones were used where hoggin, earth or sand would have been satisfactory. On his advice a Sub-surveyor 'who has been properly instructed in the science of road making' was appointed at a salary of a guinea and a half a week, who would live in the town and direct work on the roads for the Commissioners under McAdam's general supervision.

From 1606, the Corporation attempted to minimise damage to roads by making bye-laws which, for instance, forbade the use of carts with iron-shod wheels. Angel Hill was sometimes the cause of dispute between Corporation and parish officers, the latter claiming that it was part of the land on which the fairs and markets were held, and that the Corporation should repair it, while the Corporation argued that it was highway and should be repaired by the parishes. On more than one occasion, the Guildhall Feoffees, taking care to make it clear that they were not creating a precedent, offered to contribute to the cost of repairs if the Corporation and the two parishes would also contribute. The first instance of the use of Angel Hill instead of the older name, Mustow, is in connection with the removal of a dung hill in 1663.

A bye-law of 1607 was designed to prevent 'hogges and swyne' from roaming about the streets, and even into the churches during service time. The penalty was a fine of 4d, to be paid before any animal impounded by the beadles could be restored to its owner; the same fine was payable by those householders who failed to clean the streets and gutters outside their houses each week. Except when building work was in hand, no one was allowed to pile up such things as timber, trestles, blocks, wood or millstones in front of their houses for more than six days on pain of a fine of 3s 4d. Street lighting was also the responsibility of the residents, and all those who lived in the centre of the town were required every night in winter from All Saints day (1 November) to Candlemas (2 February) 'except the mone doth shine' to hang a lantern beside their doors from six in the evening until nine o'clock at night, on pain of a 4d fine. (These are old-style dates, and must be amended to 11 November and 12 February to conform to the Gregorian calendar we use now, as there is a difference of 20 minutes in the time of sunset in the two sets of dates.)

As wood became scarce, attempts were made to restrict its use for fuel, and brewers, dyers and others whose trades required large quantities were required to use 'sea cole', sedge or straw instead of wood or charcoal. This was a serious matter, and the fine for non-observance was £1.

After the fire of 1608, the Corporation took steps to ensure such a disaster could never recur and, in addition to forbidding the use of roofing thatch, Corporation members and those, such as brewers and maltsters, whose occupations involved a high fire risk, were required to keep in their houses a number of leather tankards or fire buckets. From time to time these had to be brought to the Guildhall for inspection, to ensure that they were in good condition.

In the eighteenth century, the insurance companies provided fire buckets for those clients whose houses were marked with fire plates, such as that still on the premises of Coral Bookmakers, in Abbeygate Street. There were parochial fire engines for both parishes by the end of the 18th century, that for St Mary's kept in the Church. The town's first fire station was opened in 1899 in the south part of the building which later became the Bury St Edmunds Library on Cornhill.

In monastic times the men of Bury St Edmunds did not have to go outside the town to obtain justice, all cases being heard in the Abbot's courts, while the Abbot's overriding authority within the town ensured that the King's courts for the shire, ie assizes and quarter sessions, never sat in Bury St Edmunds before the dissolution. At first, assizes were held at Catteshall in Great Barton and later, they were regularly held on Henhowe Heath, just north of the town. A petition survives, dated 1301-2, from the Friars of Babwell, asking the King to oppose the permanent removal of the Hall of Pleas from Catteshall to Henhowe, which was near the Friary because, when the weather was bad, the crowds assembled for the courts had flocked into their church.

In 1579, Thomas Badby gave the former monastic grammar school building to the Guildhall Feoffees for a Shire House, and some of the older Shire Hall buildings, including the courts, still stand on the site. From 1606, the Corporation appointed magistrates, called Assistants, for the town, and from 1614 held its own court of Quarter Sessions, as well as the Court of Record, which heard civil cases up to the sum of £200, the Court Leet which dealt with matters concerned with such things as weights and measures and blocked-up water courses and, during the fair, a court of Pie Powder, a commercial court (called Pie Powder from *pied poudre,* from the dusty feet of the merchants who used it) which settled disputes between visiting merchants on the spot. The Assizes were held in the town from about 1584, in which year the Guildhall Feoffees bought linen for the use of the judges; sometimes they also gave them presents when they came here in the course of their circuit. The 1607 bye-laws were approved by Sir Edward Coke and William Danyell in the course of their summer circuit in 1607. The provision of good accommodation for the Assizes was a matter of some importance as, inevitably, while the Court was in session, the town was full of litigants and their legal advisers. There were, in addition, those who, if a case of more than ordinary interest was to be heard, merely turned up as spectators, to the great advantage of the traders. A threat to remove Bury from the circuit was more than once sufficient to ensure that funds were found to improve the Shire Hall.

The most famous case heard in Bury St Edmunds was the trial of William Corder for the murder of Maria Marten in the Red Barn at Polstead, the basis for the famous melodrama, *Maria Marten and the Red Barn.* Another celebrated case, heard in March 1721/2, was that in which Arundel Coke, a barrister and one of the Guildhall Feoffees, paid his handy-man to murder his brother-in-law, Edward Crisp, so as to get his hands on Crisp's estates which would have been inherited by Coke's wife. The murder attempt failed, but Coke was convicted of slitting Edward Crisp's nose. Crisp lived at 6, Angel Hill (the Tourist Information Centre) and Arundel Coke in the house now called St Denys on the east corner of Honey Hill and Sparhawk Street, while the attempted murder took place in the churchyard.

The prison on the west side of Cornhill used by the Abbot before the dissolution formed part of the property granted to the Corporation in 1608, and a prison on this site was used by the County, as well as the Borough Magistrates, until 1805. When the new Gaol in Sicklesmere Road was opened, it was in the charge of a remarkable Gaol Keeper called John Orridge, who influenced the design adopted and was later asked to design a model prison (based on Bury Gaol) for the Czar of Russia. Moyses Hall, from about 1626, was used by the Borough Magistrates as a bridewell and later, as a police station, until 1892, when the police moved into the St John's Street Police Station. The first report of the Town's Watch Committee, dated 29 February 1836, recommended that a police force should be established and that a room in Moyses Hall should be used as a 'Station House'; previously, constables had been elected for each ward by the Court Leet.

Before the dissolution of the Abbey, the Abbot had sat as a peer in Parliament, but it was only in 1614 that the Corporation acquired the right to return two members, who were elected by the thirty seven Corporation members alone; for many years those chosen were the nominees of the Duke of Grafton and the Earl (later Marquess) of Bristol. Despite the small number of electors, it could, nevertheless, be an expensive matter treating them and their dependents, until they could be relied upon to vote as their political patrons required. For instance, on New Year's Day 1759, Admiral Hervey, whose portrait by Sir Joshua Reynolds now hangs in the Manor House, spent nearly £400 entertaining about 360 people at the Angel! One famous member for Bury St Edmunds was John, Lord Hervey, author of the *Memoirs of the Court of George II*; another was Augustus Henry, 3rd Duke of Grafton, who was Prime Minister from 1766-1770. The introduction of a wider franchise in 1832 was heralded by a riot when supporters of Francis King Eagle, the radical candidate, attacked the house of Philip James Case, a local attorney who was the Registrar of the Archdeaconry of Sudbury and one of the Corporation members. Case panicked and fired a fowling piece into the crowd and, inevitably, someone was hurt.

Before the passing of the Ballot Act in 1872, voting took place in a specially erected booth outside the Angel Hotel, where those who were entitled to vote had their name and votes (for two members were returned for the Borough until 1885) recorded in the poll book, which was usually published soon afterwards. William Spanton's photograph of voting in progress in 1865 is unusual, if not unique.

Gradually all the modern services which we take for granted were introduced into Bury St Edmunds. In 1820, an Act was obtained authorising the lighting of the town by gas, and the gas works were opened in Teyfen Road in 1834. The Paving Commissioners began a water undertaking, which was originally used for street cleansing, in 1858, and the water works tanks, which were constructed on the Corporation yard site in 1864, can be seen in a photograph taken from the spire of St John's Church, when it was in scaffolding after it had been struck by lightning on 27 May 1871. A pumping station was built in 1881 and, at one time, a windmill was used to lift water. The water tower in West Road, which is a dominant feature of the skyscape of the western part of the town, was built in 1952. A sewage farm was constructed at West Stow in 1885.

The first newspaper to be published in Bury St Edmunds was *The Suffolk Mercury* or *St Edmundsbury Post* which was produced from 1714 until about 1740. Its local content was mainly advertisements. Rather more news of a local nature is to be found in the *Bury Post*, 1782-5, which was continued as the *Bury and Norwich Post* until it was incorporated in the *Bury Free Press* from the beginning of January 1932. The *Post* and the *Free Press*, which was first published on 14 July 1855, provide the local historian with an excellent source over a long period; historians of tomorrow will miss the verbatim reports of speeches which enable one to gauge local feeling on many matters.

For a long time, Bury St Edmunds was a garrison town. The Suffolk Regiment was originally part of the 12th Regiment of Foot, which was raised in 1685, and had as its badge a Castle and Key with the words 'Gibraltar, 1779-83', in recognition of the distinguished part the regiment played in the siege of Gibraltar. The Regiment added the words 'East Suffolk' to its number in 1782, and began to foster good relations with the county, as a help in recruiting. After the Caldwell Reform of the Army, it became the Suffolk Regiment on 1 July 1881, the 3rd Battalion being the West Suffolk Militia. More recently, the Suffolk Regiment was amalgamated with the Royal Norfolks to form the East Anglian Regiment while, from 1 September 1964, the Suffolk

Regiment has been the 1st Battalion of the Royal Anglian Regiment. The town became 32nd Infantry Brigade Depôt in 1873 and in 1878 the Gibraltar Barracks were built in Out Risbygate as the Headquarters of the 12th regimental district, with accommodation for 250 men and with 32 married quarters. The north chancel chapel of St Mary's Church is the Regimental Chapel of the Suffolk Regiment and was furnished for this purpose to designs of Sir Ninian Comper in 1935. Many people still recollect how large crowds would follow the soldiers, with their band, back to the barracks after the Sunday morning church parade.

The Suffolk Yeomanry was founded in 1793 by Arthur Young, the celebrated agriculturalist, who lived at Bradfield Combust Hall. Originally there were four troops of light dragoons of which the 4th Troop was at Bury, commanded by Capt Lord Charles Brome, afterwards Lord Cornwallis; their function was to afford home defence against possible invasion by the French. By 1814 there were eight independent troops which were then formed into the 1st Regiment Loyal Suffolk Yeomanry Cavalry, of which the 4th troop was still based at Bury St Edmunds. After a period of suspension from 1827-1831, the independent troops were re-formed, the first troop being at Bury St Edmunds as heavy dragoons instead of the original light dragoons. These were amalgamated in 1875 as the Royal Suffolk Hussars. After the Duke of York, later King George V, had reviewed the Hussars at their centenary parade on Angel Hill in 1893, he conferred upon them the title the 'Duke of York's Own Loyal Suffolk Hussars'. The Regiment (by then the 358th (Suffolk Yeomanry) Medium Regiment, RA(TA) was granted the freedom of the Borough of Bury St Edmunds on 19 September 1953, and was amalgamated with the Norfolk Yeomanry to form 308 (Suffolk & Norfolk Yeomanry) Field Regiment, RA(TA) on 1 May 1961.

Bury St Edmunds and Westgate (Brewery) Fire Brigades, 1 November 1936. In front at the left is Mr Bloomfield, Chief of the Westgate (Brewery) Fire Brigade. In front of the extending ladder are a Borough fireman; Mr R.H. Beaumont, Borough Surveyor; the Mayor, Mr. F.S. Bright; a Westgate fireman; J.B. Parkington, Chairman of the Watch Committee; E.L.D. Lake of Greene, King & Son: a Borough fireman; Chief Officer Groves of the Borough Fire Brigade. (OGJ)

LEFT: A wind pump in the Corporation yard which was used to raise water. The photograph, which dates from about 1911, shows the spire of St John's church in the background. (SRO(B)) BELOW: On the left, Shire Hall (with columns) built 1841-2 and rebuilt in 1907; the Magpie Inn, demolished 1871, in the centre and the Manor House, right, called the Court House at this time as it was used as the Judges' Lodgings during assizes. (JK)
RIGHT: Title page of the account of the trial of Arundel Coke, 1721. (SRO(B))

Electors Names.	The Honourable Augustus John Hervey Esqr	Sr Robert Davers Bart
Robert Hawes		Robt Hawes
John Mills	Jno. Mills	
James Sturgeon	James Sturgeon	
Peast Hart		P. Hart
William Cass	William Cass	
Neale Ward		Neale Ward
John Siday		
John Jaye	Jno Jaye	
John Eldred	John Eldred	
Orbell Ray		Orbell Ray
William Robards		Wm Robards
Thomas Complin		Thos Complin
Thomas Johnson	Thos Johnson	
Peter Rogers		Peter Rogers
Samuel Harrison		Sam: Harrison
John Challis	John Challis	
Joshua Grigby		Josa Grigby
John Hallo		
James Oakes Gent		James Oakes
Edward Isaack Jackson Gent	Edwd Is. Jackson	
Sr Samuel Prime Knt		
The Honble Thos Hervey Esqr	Thos Hervey	
William Allen Gent	Wm Allen	
Lawrence Wright Esqr Coroner	Law Wright	

Concerning the Election of
St. Edmunds Bury
In SUFFOLKE.

AT the Election were Competitors, Sir *Thomas Cullum* Baronet, deceased, *John Rotheram* Esquire, Sir *Thomas Harvey*, *Thomas Jermyn* Esquire.

Sir *Thomas Cullum*, and Mr. *Rotheram*, were chosen by the major part of free Burgesses; but the Alderman of the Burrough unduely returned Sir *Thomas Harvey* and Mr. *Jermyn*.

The Cause is to be heard on Wednesday the first of *December*, 1680.

St. Edmunds-Bury is a Burrough by Prescription, and had ancient Writs & Precepts to Elect, before any Grant from the Crown.

The King recites, that *Bury* is an Ancient Burrough, and Creates Twelve Capital Burgesses, and Twenty four of the Common Council.

The King grants that there shall be Two Burgesses in Parliament, and that the Alderman and chief Burgesses, and Burgesses of the Common Council, shall choose them and keep them at the Charge of the said Burrough.

Sir *Tho. Harvey*, and Mr. *Jermyn*, are Chosen by the Select Number.

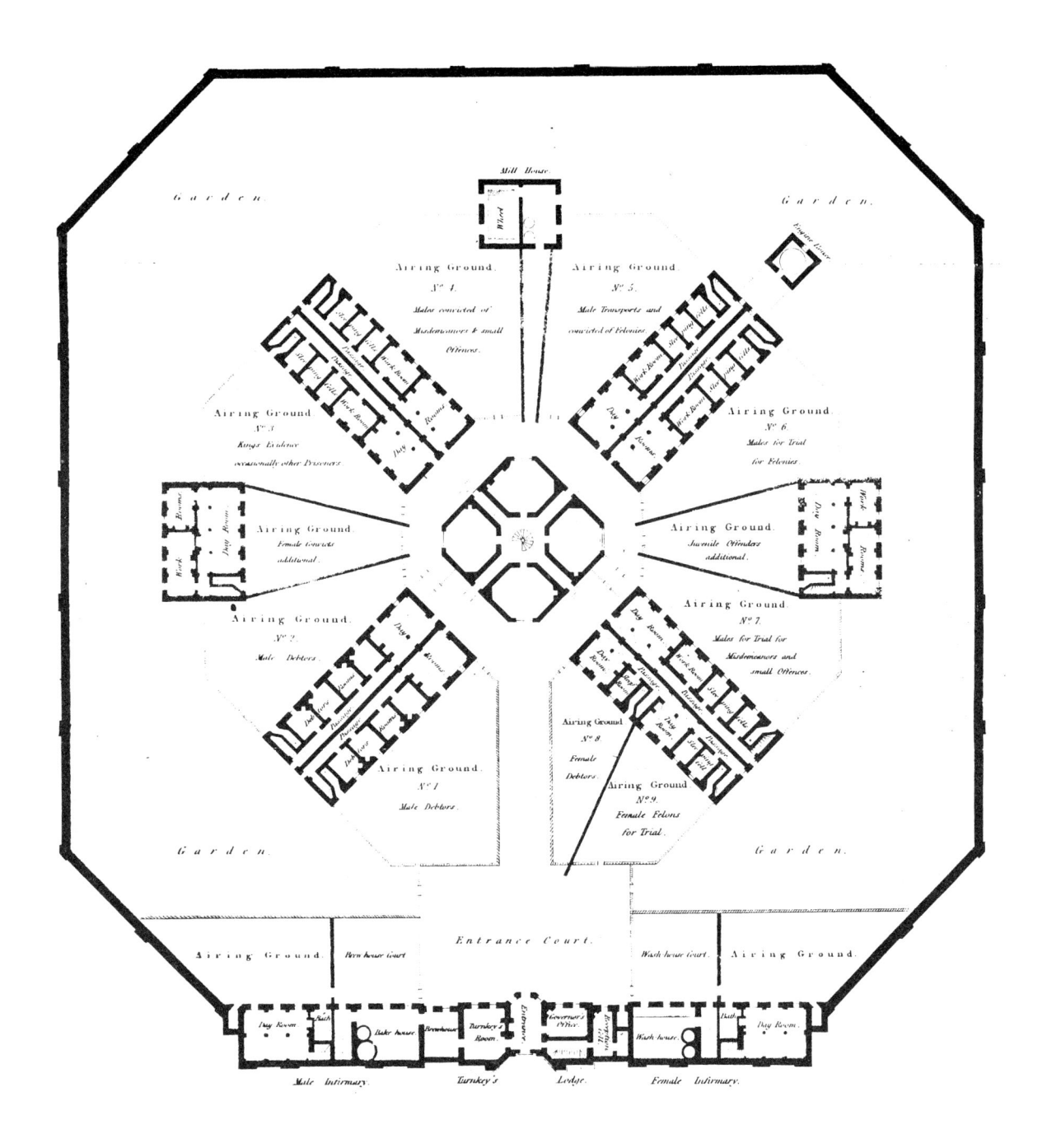

OPPOSITE ABOVE LEFT: An engraving showing Arundel Coke's attack on Mr Crisp.(OGJ) RIGHT: A voting paper with the names of the 37 Corporation members, indicating how they voted for a member to replace Augustus Henry Fitzroy, who had become Duke of Grafton, in 1757.(SRO(B)) BELOW LEFT: Notice that a case was to be heard on 1 December 1680 about the Bury election in which the freemen had asserted a right to vote.(SRO(I)) RIGHT: Unusually, the Corporation instructed the members on their views when the abolition of slavery was discussed, no doubt under the influence of Thomas Clarkson.(SRO(B)) ABOVE: The county gaol in Sicklesmere Road (now called The Fort) was designed by George Byfield in 1805 and enlarged under the supervision of William Wilkins in 1821, to incorporate most of the additional features advocated by John Orridge, the Governor when he designed a prison for the Emperor of Russia.(SRO(B))

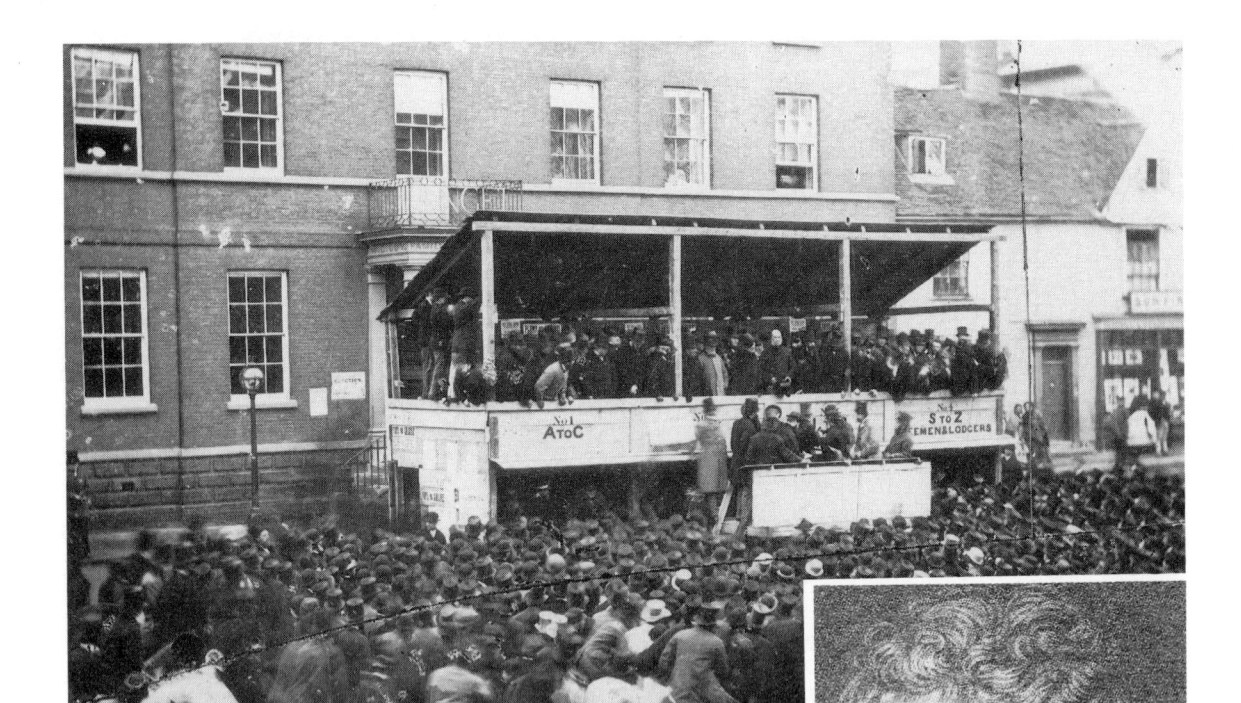

Hardcastle—Plumpers, 107.

Abbot Frederick Ablett, Angel hill
Allen James, Raingate street
Bailey James, Eastgate street
Barrett John, Cotton lane
Baker William, Corn market
Brewster Henry, Guildhall street
Bigge Jessie Edward, Brentgovel st.
Bear Thomas Mayhew, Corn market
Balaam Charles, Whiting street
Biles George, Whiting street
Bullock Walter, Mustow street
Barnard Benjamin, Butts
Britton John, St. John's street
Brewster John, Southgate street
Barton Frederick, Churchgate street
Barton John, College street
Collins Thomas, St. Mary's square
Cornish Simeon, Meat Market
Carter William Henry, St. John's st.
Catling Charles, Union terrace
Clark Robert, Meat market
Cooper Thomas White, Meat market
Death Daniel, Southgate street
Downs The man of the street
Drake John, Short Brackland
Densley John, Whiting street
Ely John, Cemetery road
Elam Edward, Eastgate street
Fenton Reuben, St. Andrew's street
Frost Joseph, Sparhawk street
Freelove William, Guildhall street
Goff Ezekiel, Mustow street
Graves Edward, Churchgate street
Gates Waite, Southgate street
Golding Simon, Cemetery road
Goddard Abner, Victoria street
Goodwin Robert, Horringer road
Gilson Thomas, Whiting street
Head Henry William, Abbeygate st.
Hirst Joseph, Whiting street
Huscroft John, St. John's street
Hawkes John, Whiting street
Holden Michael, Hatter street
Hooper John Alfred, Barn's lane
Harrold William Bruce, Out Westgate
Howe Thomas, Southgate street
Jennings Thomas, Union terrace
Jenner Charles Samuel, Westgate st.
Jennings Edward, Raingate street

Catton Charles, Crown street
Chapman Thomas, St. John's street
Childs George, Guildhall street
Clarke George, Crown street
Clayton Kid Edmund, Guildhall street
Cockendge William, Tay Fen road
Collins Robert, College street
Orick James, St. John's Street
Cooper William, Well street
Cullum Charles, Long Brackland
Clements Samuel, Churchgate street
Cullum John, Long Brackland
Crassweller Wm. Ellis, Abbeygate st.
Cornish George, Whiting street
Collis Wm. Humphrey, Abbeygate st.
Clarke Alfred Michael, Abbeygate st.
Clark John, Crown street
Clarke Frederick, Union terrace
Clarke James, College street
Cowell George, Westgate street
Coates James Steel, St. Andrew's st
Crack Walter, Meat market
Crack William, Traverse
Clark Samuel John, Crown street
Clay George Pearson, Guildhall street
Clodd Mrtn.Cottingham, Northgate st.
Double George Scarfe, Cemetery road
Doe John, Angel hill
Death Edward, jun., St. John's street
Daines William, St. John's street
Day Thomas, Abbeygate street
Drake William, Mill lane
Dawes James, Mill lane
Earl Richard, Garland street
Everard Charles, Westgate street
Ely Joseph, Out Westgate
Edwards Robert, Out Westgate
Fletcher Robert, Southgate street
Fowler James, Out Westgate
Frost James, Cemetery road
Fordham Frederick, Bridewell lane
Fitch John Barnard, Corn market
Frost Henry, College street
Foreman John, Crown street
Gooch William, Southgate street
Greene Edward Walter, Westgate st.
Gross William, Chequer square
Garwood Thomas, Out Northgate
Goldsmith Harry, Risbygate street
Gross Samuel, Westgate street
Gray George, Abbeygate street
Goold Richard, Whiting street

Scotcher John Adams, Meat market
Spalding Robert, Union terrace
Spooner John, Churchgate street
Sparks George, Guildhall street
Syrett William, Hatter street
Smith John, Out Westgate
Sawyer James, Churchgate street
Salmon William, Guildhall street
Sewell Robert, Saint John's street
Salter Robert, Northgate street
Tozer Charles James, Garland street
Towler Edward, Saint John's street
Taylor Thomas, Barn's lane
Taylor Charles Henry, Low Baxter st.
Theobald Frederick, Brentgovel street
Thomas Edward Charles, Churchyard
Wilkin Algernon, Guildhall street
Wollaston Charles, Northgate street
Wells Edward Cornish, Crown street
Walden George, Schoolhall street
Weston Robert John, Risbygate street
Williams William, Angel hill
Warren William, St. Andrew's street
Whipps George, Long Brackland
Warner Jas. A., Short Brackland
Watling William Cain, Cemetery road
Wylie Theophilus, Whiting st.
White Charles, Southgate street
Weldhen William, Southgate street
Wallis Benjamin, Garland street
Wade Robert, Brentgovel street

Hervey—Plumpers, 44.

Andrews Fredk. Chas., Guildhall st.
Beevor Wm. Smythies, Northgate st.
Borton John Henry, Hatter street
Bevan William Robert, Whepstead
Blake Thomas Gage, Eastgate street
Bevan Beckford, Northgate street
Bevan Jas. Johnstone, Northgate st.
Blake George, Eastgate street
Bonfellow Edmund, Butter market
Crack William, Honey hill
Clarke John William, Whiting street
Cockrill William, Horringer road
Cares R. Martin, Little Whelnetham
Frewer William, Chequer square
Frost Daniel, Well street
Guy William George, Angel hill
Goodwin John Wycliff, Angel hill
Gates Robert Peter, Union terrace

Edgar Robert
Emerson James
Fenton George
Fletcher Fred
Fenton William
Foreman James
Fuller William
Goodrich Joseph
Gurney Fred
Guy John H
Greene Joseph
Gardener He
Harvey Robert
Howe Robert
Hubbard William
Houghton William
Harpley Charles
Hunter John,
Hempstead J
Harris John,
Hubbard George
Hall Edward,
Hardwick John
Head Richard
Hutton Hugh
Hooper William
Harris Henry
Hunter Arthur
Jennings Benjamin
Leech Charles
Le Grice Hen
Limmer Wm.
Lockwood Jas
Limmer James
Le Butt Josiah
Lanham George
Last Wm. Ne
Last James, Abbeygate street
Lankester Frederic, Abbeygate street
Lease Chas. Frederick, Out Risbygate
Lagden Robert, College street
Lucia Thomas Fraucis, Abbeygate st.
Major Josiah, Abbeygate street
Mothersole William, Albert street
Manning William, Prospect row
Murton Joseph, Hatter street
Major William, Traverse
Marriott Benjamin, Out Risbygate
Mayfield Myas, Mustow street
Merrell Joseph, Guildhall street
Makin Henry, St Mary's square
Morris John, Garland street

Hervey and Greene, 53.

Andrews Alfred, St. John's street
Barrell Roberts, Westley
Bullen Charles Henry, Butter market
Coe Walter, St. Andrew's street
Coe John, Guildhall street
Death Edward, Southgate street
Darkin James, Out Westgate
Dalson Rowland, Whiting street
Darkin John, Out Westgate
Ellis John, Guildhall street
Edwards Henry, Union terrace
Ellis Thomas, Brentgovel street

ABOVE: An unusual, perhaps unique, photograph of the hustings, 1865. BELOW: Part of the poll for the 1865 election, the last but one before the introduction of the secret ballot.(SRO(B)) INSET: Peter Gedge, who founded *The Bury Post* in 1782. His obituary in *The Morning Chronicle*, 19 January 1818 stated that his paper was 'distinguished by its firm and consistent avowal of the principles of civil and religious liberty, in a place noted for aristocratical ignorance and pride...The Corporation of Bury is notoriously venal. "Loaves and Fishes" should be its motto.'(SRO(B)) OPPOSITE ABOVE: Col and Mrs Guinness outside the Angel, in a carriage decorated for an election, in the early years of this century. (SRO(B)) BELOW: The Suffolk Yeomanry Cavalry on centenary parade, 1893.(OGJ)

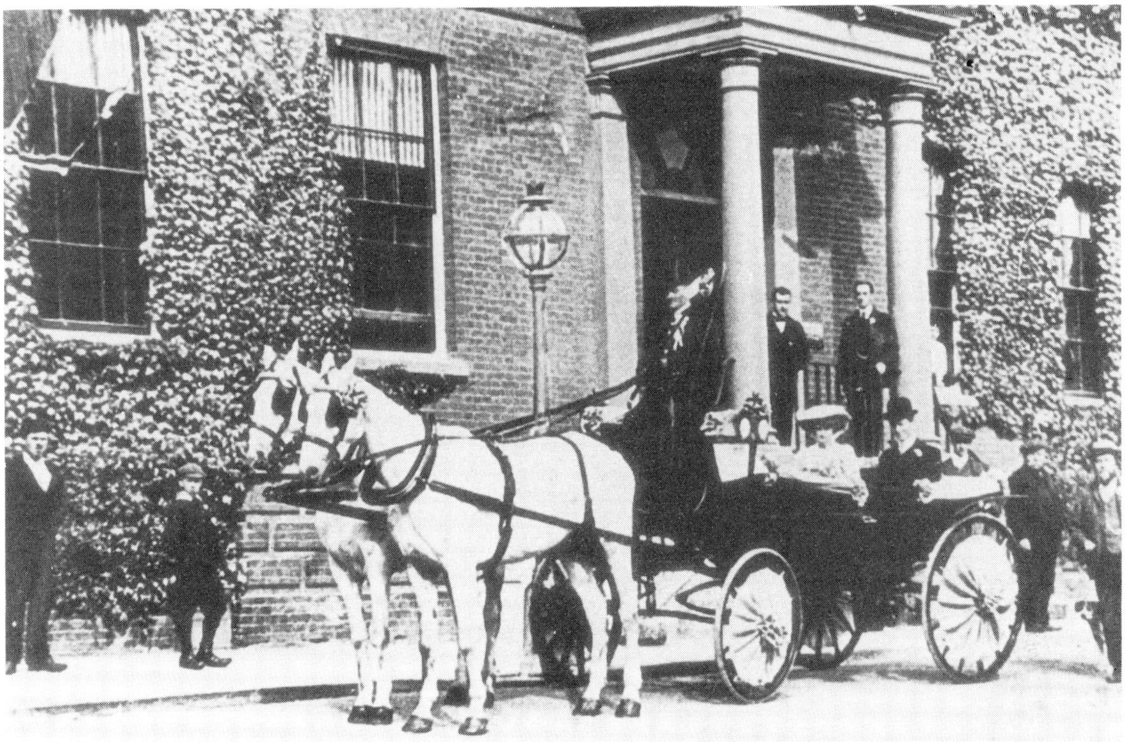

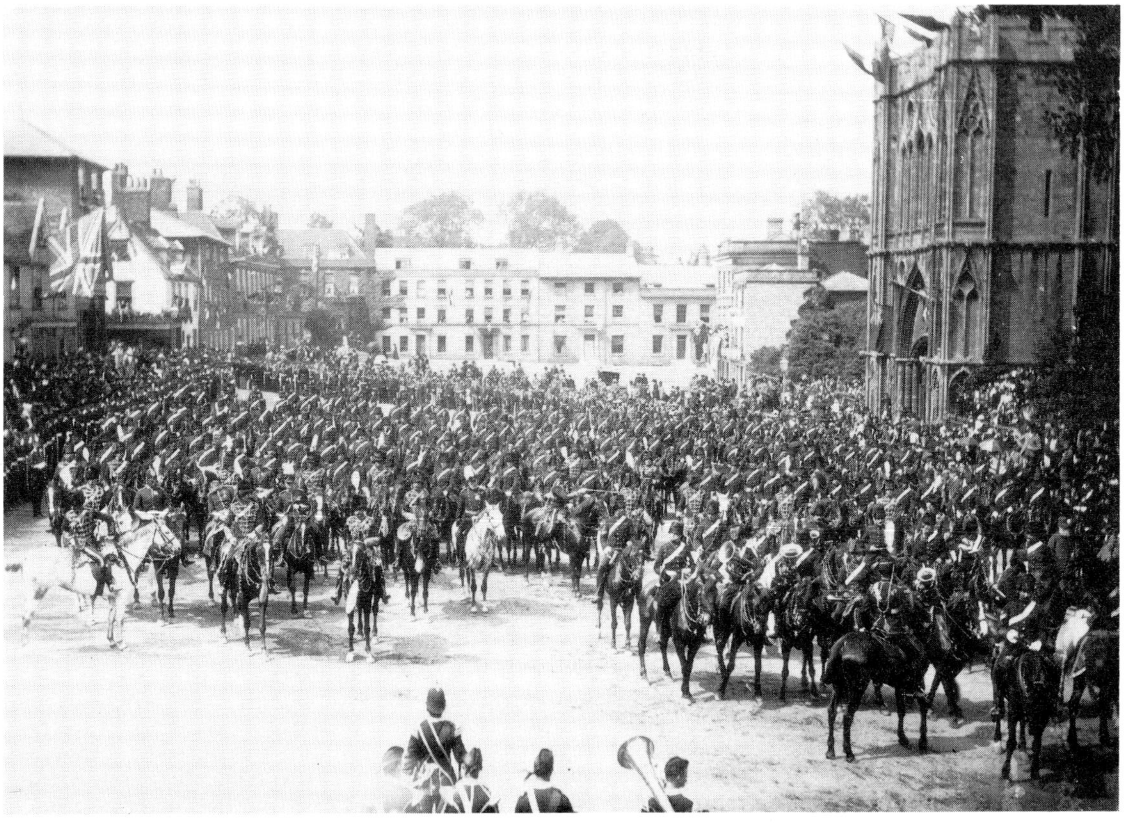

ABOVE: Damage in the Butter Market after a Zeppelin raid, 1916.(OGJ) BELOW: Members of the Royal Observer Corps at the Group Operations Room in the Guildhall, c1949, when a presentation was made to Observer Thelma Musk as she was about to emigrate to the USA. Included in the photograph are Observer Moore, Observer Musk, Chief Observer Phyllis Cooper, Observer Leathers, Mrs Beryl Fulcher (a former Mayoress whose husband was a Duty Controller) and Observer Officer Frank Williams (also a Duty Controller and for many years the representative of the *East Anglian Daily Times* in the town).(SRO(B))

Burye Worke

Since before the Norman Conquest, Bury St Edmunds has been an important market centre for West Suffolk and its convenient position, at the centre of a network of roads, was strengthened by the Abbey, which jealously guarded the rights of its market and took vigorous action to put down rivals. The Sacrist was the clerk of the market and the tolls are accounted for in his surviving account rolls; after the dissolution, the right to hold the market was surrendered to the Crown, which let it for terms of years until it was acquired by the Corporation. While the provision market still attracts crowds into the Cornhill and Butter Market each Wednesday and Saturday the Cattle Market was moved from a site near the Corn Exchange to St Andrews Street in 1828; this is now part of the car park, but the attractive toll collector's booth still stands. The move from Cornhill was not popular, and the first market on the new site saw a disturbance, if not a riot, and the Town Clerk narrowly escaped injury when an inebriated farmer from Ixworth Thorpe hurled a brick at him. Later, the Cattle Market spread to adjacent areas of St Andrews Street, and eventually purpose-built buildings were erected for the convenience of the auctioneers.

The Corn Market has always been important. In 1583, the Guildhall Feoffees raised the money to build a 'very fayer large house for cornesellers . . . wherein they may stande to their great ease verye comodiouslye in the heate of Somer and also in the tyme of reynye and cold wet winter' to replace a simple stone cross, the stones of which were sold for £2, which had hitherto marked the site of the market. It is not known where the 1583 Market Cross stood, but it was destroyed in the fire of 1608 and a timber cross was built to replace it, on a site which had formerly been part of Rotten Row. In 1774, the Corporation faced the south front of the Cross to a design of Robert Adam and then proceeded to encase the whole building, the ground floor being open for the corn dealers, apart from two small shops at the north end. By the beginning of the 19th century, the Market Cross was too small and, in 1836, the Town Council built a new Corn Exchange; this building (formerly the Library and recently converted into shops) had become too small by 1862, when the present Corn Exchange was built.

Mediaeval Bury St Edmunds provided work for traders and craftsmen of many kinds, but it was the clothmaking industry on which the town's early prosperity largely depended. Clothmaking required workers skilled in many crafts, and the town abounded with weavers of various kinds of cloth, fullers, shearmen and many other tradesmen, workers in all these trades being supplied with raw materials and paid by clothiers, who organised the whole operation and sold the finished product. Crafts such as spinning were usually carried on by the workers in their own cottages, so a spinning house such as that which John Baret had in his house in Chequer Square in 1463 is unusual. Quite a lot of weavers were described as dornix or darnick weavers (derived from the Flemish word for Tournay) which seems to have been a fabric used for hangings and, sometimes, ecclesiastical vestments. Bury St Edmunds was famous for its coverlet weaving, and names of those who followed this trade are often encountered, while Adam Browne of Brandon, who made his will on 19 January 1550/1 mentions 'a coverlett of Burye worke'.

As the Abbot and Convent controlled the market, so it controlled trade and the craft guilds within the town. References to craft guilds in mediaeval Bury St Edmunds are rare, but this may be because the relevant documents have been lost, not because there were few such guilds. The earliest guild of which there is a note was that of the bakers, which was established between 1166 and 1180, for during those years Abbot Hugh I granted privileges which prevented any who were not members of the guild from baking bread for sale without the consent of the fraternity. Such people were punished by a fine of twenty shillings, half of which went to the Sacrist and the other half to the guild, just as happened when members of the guild were fined for breaking the assize of bread, which controlled the quality and price of this essential commodity.

The cordwainers or shoemakers also had a guild, as is shown by a deed dated 1266 by which Geoffrey the Porter, the son of Roger the Porter, conveyed to the guild a shop with buildings in Cordwainers Street (which was somewhere in the market place, the exact site unknown) for the use of the fraternity for ever. In view of the importance of clothmaking, it is not surprising to find that the third craft guild of which we know is that of the linen and woollen weavers, whose new rules, drawn up in 1477, survive among the Borough's records. They were approved by the Bailiffs, who were the Sacrist's officers and, when fines were imposed for breach of the rules, half the sum paid found its way into the Sacrist's coffers.

Twenty seven of the bye-laws drawn up in 1607 relate to the activities of the bakers and, while some 'companie or societie or fellowshipp' of bakers was envisaged and was to be approved by the Alderman and Burgesses, it is not clear whether the mediaeval bakers' guild survived the dissolution. Members had to be freemen of the Borough and, of course, had to keep the assize of bread, but other rules intended to prevent 'foreign' bakers from trading in the town, except under strict control by the authorities, required each baker to mark his loaves with his own mark, and insisted that no baker should have more than one stall in the market; the baker's stalls were to be allocated according to the seniority of the bakers in the company. The only other company mentioned in these bye-laws is that of the linen weavers. In both cases, fines levied from breach of the bye-laws were to be divided into three parts: one for the use of the company concerned, one for the Alderman and Burgesses, and the third for the poor people of the town. An attempt to set up a company of clothiers in 1609 was short-lived and did nothing to improve the declining fortunes of those who were engaged in weaving broadcloth, a fine, twilled woollen cloth (so called by this date for its quality rather than its width) on which Bury's mediaeval prosperity was largely based.

By the early years of the 17th century, Bury St Edmunds, with a population of over 5,000 was, to use a modern term, a depressed area. Bury St Edmunds has for so long been a quiet market town that it is difficult for us to appreciate that in the late mediaeval period it was a large manufacturing town. Broadcloth weaving was in decline by the beginning of the 17th century and one of the few surviving contemporary orders of the Corporation relates to an attempt to introduce the weaving of the new draperies, a lighter type of fabric then fashionable and, because it was largely made in Norwich, sometimes called Norwich stuff. Dated 26 October 1622 it reads 'At this assembly it was agreed, that for as much as it is earnestly desyred that provision may be made to sett the pore of this towne on worke as well for the preventing of Idlenes as of *[a]* meanes to sett them on worke, that the trade of making and weaving of stuffes which is hopped wilbe beneficiall to the poore sort of this towne shalbe labored to be brought to this towne, and that sufficient men, either F*[lemings,?]* Frence men or Dutchman *[sic]* if they may be gotten to come from Norwich which are skylfull in the making of Norwich stuffes to set up in this towne the sayd trade, with this causion that the sayd persons *[?]* which shall com from Norwich come as singly as may be without married Jurnyemen'. The Corporation were determined to do all that they could to limit the number of hungry mouths which had to be fed in Bury St Edmunds.

The 1607 bye-laws show that only those who were freemen of the Borough were entitled to set up in business. Throughout the 17th century and into the 18th, the freedom was essential for anyone who intended to trade in Bury St Edmunds but, as the 18th century wore on, fewer men were admitted to the freedom and, by the turn of the 19th century (apart from attorneys who wished to practise in the Borough Courts), only those who had ambitions to become Corporation members sought the freedom.

Brewing has long been of great importance to the local economy and today Greene King is one of the twelve major breweries in the country and, of course, a major employer, with its buildings in the historic heart of the town. Neither 1799, the date everyone knows from the firm's beer mats, nor 1800, the date above the door of the head office in Westgate Street, are necessarily the date when Benjamin Greene started brewing at the Westgate Street brewery, which had been run by the Wright family for much of the 18th century; he and his partner William Buck first advertised in *The Bury and Norwich Post* in April 1806. In 1877 came the merger with the St Edmund brewery, which was run by Fred King, and since then the firm has gone from strength to strength to reach its present position among East Anglian and national breweries; its products are known as far away as California. The influence of the brewery can be felt in many aspects of town life.

Equally based on the agriculture of the surrounding countryside is the British Sugar Corporations factory in Hollow Road, which was opened in 1925. Tate and Lyle were instrumental in setting up the factory which, with 17 others, was amalgamated into the British Sugar Corporation Ltd under the Sugar Industry Act. The sugar beet silos, and the Maltings of ABM nearby dominate the skyline and, if the ABM building is sometimes referred to as the 'Concrete Cathedral', it is appropriate that this vast building should reflect a trade well established in the town by the 17th century and an important factor in its economy for centuries.

In the days of Robert Boby and Son and of Cornish and Lloyd Ltd, the making of agricultural implements was also important. Robert Boby was a retail ironmonger who invented a machine to separate chaff from corn, and found it so popular that he eventually gave up his shop and devoted the rest of his career to manufacturing agricultural, brewing and malting machinery. The firm Robert Boby Ltd was founded in 1856, became a limited liability company in 1898 and part of the Vickers Group in 1925. The Boby works in St Andrews Street closed in 1971, but one of the Boby buildings has recently been re-erected at the Museum of East Anglian Life at Stowmarket.

From early times the town has had its professional men; the great Abbot Baldwin himself was a celebrated physician, and, as the years go by, it becomes easier to find more and more physicians and surgeons who have practised in the town. There were also lawyers in the town from an early date and John Mallowes, the first Town Clerk, is a typical example of a busy country town lawyer involved in many local activities in addition to his practice. The Grigbys - three generations of Joshuas - were a local legal dynasty in the eighteenth century, the last of whom became MP for Suffolk and lived at Drinkstone Park. Among those who were Recorder of Bury St Edmunds are a number of distinguished lawyers, including Sir Thomas Richardson. He was Recorder in the 1620s and Speaker of the House of Commons in 1621. He made his mark on legal history in 1628, when he refused to allow John Felton, a member of a distinguished Suffolk family who assassinated the Duke of Buckingham, to be racked to obtain evidence; he thus became the first judge to rule that evidence given after the witness had been tortured was inadmissible.

James Oakes, 1741-1829, is a good example of a local banker; he started life as a yarn merchant, became a tax gatherer and ended his long and active life at the head of a bank which is still represented by the Butter Market branch of Lloyds. For a time the Oakes family were in partnership with the Bevans, another prominent local family, especially in the last century, and this bank has an unusual sign with an oak tree for the founder and a bee-hive symbolising the Bevans.

Like many prosperous market towns, Bury St Edmunds had its fair share of old-established shops, of which Thomas Ridley, the grocer was, until it closed in October 1996, a good example. There has probably been a grocer's shop on that site on the corner of Abbeygate Street and Angel Lane at least from the latter part of the 17th century. The first Ridley to trade there took over from E. Ely in 1801; Thomas Ridley may have been trading as a grocer elsewhere in the town before moving up into what one might call the Bond Street of Bury St Edmunds. In addition to groceries, they had a considerable business in oils and colours, and customers from as far afield as Yorkshire, Lancashire and Nottinghamshire bought large quantities of comey ash; no-one yet knows how this was used. Another long-established Abbeygate Street shop was Quants, the shoe shop. Not many of those who, as children, wore Start-rite shoes know that they were patented by one of the Quants who owned this shop. This shop is still a shoe shop, now Dudley Mason.

The Market Cross, built soon after the fire in 1608, already had its 'lanthorn and dial' when Celia Fiennes visited the town in 1698.(St E)

ABOVE: The Market Place as it appeared c1700, showing Cupola House, built by Thomas Macro in 1693, on the right. Prior to 1828, the cattle market was held near the Corn Exchange site, as shown in this view.(SRO(B)) BELOW: Another view of about the same date clearly shows the row of inns which led to this part of the market being called 'the inns'. The buildings on the left probably include the gaol and gaol-keeper's house.(JK)

LEFT: Robert Adam's design for the south front of the Market Cross, 1774. It is said that the main beams of the timber building were found when the building was altered in the early 1970s.(St E) RIGHT: A water colour of the shambles which formerly stood on part of the Corn Exchange site. It seems to be signed G. Scharf and dated 1817.(SRO(B)) BELOW: Design for the Corn Exchange, c1862.(SRO(B))

ABOVE: Market day, c1865.(OGJ) BELOW: A market day scene at the turn of the century.(OGJ)

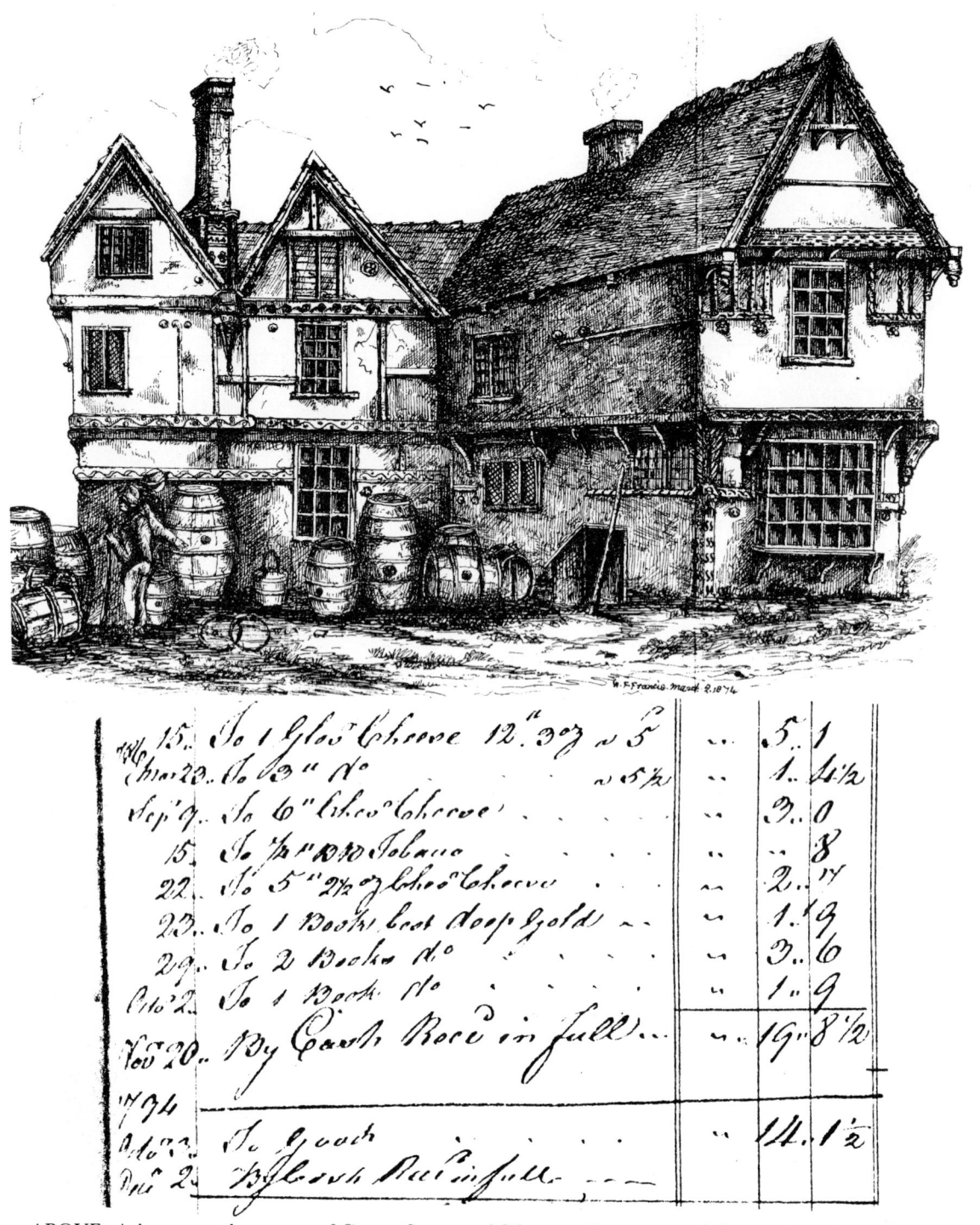

ABOVE: A house on the corner of Crown Street and Westgate Street, occupied at various times, first by Benjamin, and then by Edward Greene, between 1806 and 1853. It was pulled down in 1855 to make way for expansion of the brewery. It is thought to be that in which John Reve, the last Abbot, died and it certainly belonged to the Heighams, a family with which he had connections. BELOW: Ridley's, or possibly their forerunners in the business, dealt in oils and colours as well as groceries. John Rackham, the bookseller and binder, bought the gold leaf for his binding as well as his cheese and tobacco from them.(SRO(B))

ABOVE: A group of customers in the north and Midlands bought comey ash in large quantities at considerable cost from Ridley's. What this was and how it was used no-one knows. (SRO(B)) BELOW: Ridley's shop and staff c1900. The shop no longer deals in oils and colours. There has probably been a grocer's shop on this site since the end of the 17th century. Ridley's shop closed October 1996. (OGJ)

This Photograph of *"THE OLD CURIOSITY SHOP,' BURY ST. EDMUNDS,* will be valued by many who remember the place in its prime. It was owned and occupied for many years by members of the Fenton family, during which time the lines from *"The Princess"* would partly describe the beauty and charm of the contents :—

> " On the pavement lay
> Carved stones of the Abbey-ruin in the park,
> Huge Ammonites, and the first bones of Time ;
> And on the tables every clime and age
> Jumbled together ; celts and calumets,
> Claymore and snowshoe, toys in lava, fans
> Of sandal, amber, ancient rosaries,
> Laborious orient ivory sphere in sphere,
> The cursed Malayan crease, and battle clubs
> From the isles of palm."

At their present addresses, MESSRS. FENTON, invite inspection of Specimens of OLD ENGLISH AND FOREIGN POTTERY AND CHINA—COINS AND MEDALS—ARMS AND ARMOUR—IVORIES—GREEK, ROMAN AND EGYPTIAN ANTIQUITIES—NEOLITHIC AND PALÆOLITHIC IMPLEMENTS, and many other classes of objects interesting alike to the student, the artist, and the antiquary.

Messrs. FENTON,
"The Old Curiosity Shop,"
12, BOOKSELLER'S ROW, STRAND, W.C.
AND
ABBEYGATE STREET, BURY ST. EDMUNDS.

ABOVE: The Old Curiosity Shop c1865, on the west of Cornhill opposite the Shambles. Artist E.R. Smythe arranged these objects.(OGJ) LEFT: After leaving Cornhill, the firm had a shop in Abbeygate Street next door to Grooms, the booksellers.(OGJ) RIGHT: Several illustrations in this book are from prints by Kendall.(SRO(B))

KENDALL'S PRINT SHOP
COOK ROW, BURY.

MAY be had the most capital Historical Prints, Landscapes and Portraits, single or in volumes ; also every Assortment of Frames, Middleton's best Pencils ; Gum Elastic ; complete Sets of Water Colours ; Crayons ; genuine India Ink ; Camel's hair Pencils ; Variety of Chalks ; India Glue ; Drawing Vellum, and Paper of all Kinds ; Book of Instructions for Drawing ; Etching Tools, and burnished Plates ; Flowers of various Kinds for Ladies to draw or embroider by ; Transparent Sattin and Stuff to work upon ; great Variety of Sattin Prints for ornamenting Muffs, Work Bags, Fire-screens, Girdles, &c. Likewise Gold and Silver Spangles, Fringe, Tassels, Plate, Pearl, Shapes, Gold and Silver Chain, Cord, &c. &c.

CAMERA-OBSCURAS, PLANO-CONVEXS, and OPTIC-PILLARS.

☞ The most modern UMBRELLAS and PARISOLS.

Variety of diverting FIREWORKS, such as Crackers, Mines, Roman Candles, Chinese Fountains, Italian Suns, Wheels, Gold Flower Pots ; all of which may be discharged without the least Hazard or Danger.

GANER'S FORTE PIANOS, so distinguished for Sweetness of Tone, are Sold or Lett.

LEFT: John Deck, who kept the Post Office in the house adjoining the Norman Tower early in the 19th century, sold books and Twining's teas, as well as being agent for the Sun Fire Office.(OGJ) BELOW: Towards the end of the last century, the site of the Post Office was hotly debated; for a time it was in part of the Barclay's Bank building in Abbeygate Street, where the post carts caused much congestion. A purpose-built Post Office was opened in 1896.(OGJ) RIGHT: James Oakes, the founder of the bank which has become the Bury St Edmunds branch of Lloyds, gave the Mayor's chain in 1805. His diary is a useful source of information about political, economic and social life from 1778-1827.(St E)

ABOVE: A butcher's shop, with a window open to the elements, on the west corner of Guildhall Street and Westgate Street. It was demolished in order to widen the road in 1878.(OGJ) LEFT: Corner of Abbeygate Street and Butter Market, 1887. Note the chemist's and pawnbroker's signs.(OGJ) RIGHT: Gibbs pie shop, famous for gooseberry pies, before 1870.(OGJ)

Horringer Mill was one of a number of windmills in the town, and was demolished in c1912-1915.(OGJ)

LEFT: The first state of Kendall's print of Angel Hill shows the Angel before rebuilding; it was gabled and had a projecting sign.(SRO(B)) RIGHT: Formerly the Mermaid, the Dog and Partridge used to hold rook suppers, the rooks shot in the Churchyard.(RWE) BELOW: The 13th century Angel undercroft is now a restaurant, sketched here by John Clibbon. (JC)

For your Amusement

Originally, the inns probably afforded entertainment more to visitors than to residents. The Angel, or an inn on the same site, can claim to be the earliest recorded house. It is almost beyond doubt that an agreement made in 1281/2 between Agnes, widow of William son of Bartholomew of Bury St Edmunds on one part and Abbot John and the convent of Bury St Edmunds on the other, regarding rents from some properties in the town, refers to the 13th century undercroft now called the Vaults Restaurant; it mentions a payment of 3s 4d a year from an inn (*taberna*) held by Hugo the Taverner, at the great gate of the court of St Edmund. The same place occurs in the 1295 rental as *le taverne*, and in later rentals, such as those of 1433 and 1526 it still appears, and is without doubt part of the Castle, one of the three inns which once stood on the site of the Angel. In 1557 the Angel (with some other pieces of land) was given by William Tassell to the Guildhall Feoffees to provide money for repairing the two parish churches, for setting forth soldiers, and for the general relief of the people of the town. In 1774-1776 it was rebuilt, the architect being Mr Redgrave, and the present, quiet facade replaced the earlier gabled building, both the old and new buildings being shown in the two states of Kendall's print of Angel Hill. When it was sold by the Guildhall Feoffees on 13 August 1917 it only made £3,100.

There are many other inns of great historical interest in Bury St Edmunds. Most, perhaps all, of the inns in the market place were, of course, destroyed in the fire of 1608 and, according to a licence issued by the Alderman and Burgesses in 1611' . . . since the edefying of the howses and buildings in those places so wasted almost all the howses newly built upon those grounds and upon those places wher the said former Inns were are now converted and imployed to and for private habitacions and shoppes for Tradesmen in so much as there is greate skarsity and want in that parte of the Towne of Common Inns and necessary howses for Intertainment of Travellers and strangers which resort to the said Towne or markett . . .'. This document may well refer to the Greyhound, which was mentioned in the First Ministers' Account of the the possessions of the Abbey in 1540; the licence from which the quotation is taken was granted to Francis Pynner, then Alderman of Bury St Edmunds who, when he died in 1639, owned the Greyhound (re-named the Suffolk in the 19th century). Perhaps the reference to 'necessary howses' means public lavatories were provided in the 17th century.

There are references to the Corpus Christi procession of mystery plays in the regulations of the linen and woollen weavers drawn up in 1477—half of each fine levied from breach of the regulations was to be used to finance the pageant of 'the Assencione of oure Lord God and of the yiftys of the Holy Gost, as yt hath be customed of olde tyme owte of mynde yeerly to be had to the wurschepe of God, ammongge other payenttes in the processione in the feste of Corpus Christi'. It has been suggested that the N-town (the name of the town where the cycle was to be performed) cycle of mystery plays (so called because the banns or proclamation at the beginning read N-town rather than the names of a place) are in fact, the Bury cycle. It contains many debts to the work of

Bury's monk-poet, John Lydgate, who after all was as likely as anyone to compile a cycle for Bury St Edmunds, especially if the text was arranged for fund-raising purposes after much of the Abbey church had been destroyed by fire in 1465. A sixteenth century inventory of the Guildhall shows that the pageants, the carts on which the plays were performed, were stored there in the 1550s, though regarded as lumber. A number of play manuscripts have Bury St Edmunds associations and were collected by Cox Macro, whose family built Cupola House in the Traverse.

The new Corporation, when they drew up their code of bye-laws in 1607, provided that plays were not to be performed in inn yards or elsewhere without a licence, so we can assume that travelling companies of players were in the habit of visiting the town. Indeed, an entry in the Guildhall Feoffees' accounts for 1619 confirms this; it reads 'And of xxs given to the late Quenes (Anne of Denmark, who died 2 March 1618/19) players to send them owt of Towne when they came to playe at an unfittinge tyme'. In Shakespeare's day, inn yards with their galleries formed an ideal place for performances by travelling players, and traces of such a gallery can still be seen at the One Bull on Angel Hill. There are also remarkable photographs of the galleries at the Half Moon (which stood near to Living Department Store and W H Smith), taken before its demolition c1870. From 1639 comes the earliest reference to a play performed by the boys of the Grammar School at the Abbey, and the Governors' accounts for that year include the cost of making a stage for them, which was to be kept for future performances. This leaves unexplained what part of the Abbey site was used for this performance. Perhaps, as in 1726, a 'Great Theatrical Booth' had been erected especially for the occasion in the Abbey Yard. The Guildhall and the Shire Hall on occasions both served as makeshift playhouses, and in 1733 there were advertisements in *The Suffolk Mercury* for performances by the Norwich Company of Comedians, Servants to his Grace and Duke of Grafton, at the Play-house in the Risbygate Street.

In 1734 the Corporation made provision for both local amateur performances and for travelling companies of players when they converted the first floor of the Market Cross into a playhouse. In 1774, Robert Adam was asked by the Corporation to produce a design for the south front of the Market Cross; his drawing is titled the new theatre, not the Market Cross, and his design incorporated tragic and comic masks either side of the door. This little theatre served the town well and prospered so much, especially during the time of the Napoleonic wars, that William Wilkins, who managed the Norwich circuit of playhouses, was inspired to acquire a site in Westgate Street on which he built the Theatre Royal, whereupon the Market Cross theatre became the Concert Room. Those who played there included some of the foremost performers of their day, such as Liszt, who visited the town and gave recitals in 1842.

If the Theatre Royal's exterior is not so distinguished as that of Adam's Market Cross theatre, Wilkins' interior, which has been restored to something like its original appearance, as far as this was compatible with licensing requirements, is very fine indeed. Wilkins' success at the Market Cross theatre, which had helped to subsidise other theatres in the circuit, was not to be repeated at the New Theatre, as it was called in its early days, the result, Wilkins believed, of the 'increase of sectaries' in the town. One way or another, it operated more or less continuously until 1926, when its doors closed and, as a theatre, remained so until April Fool's day 1965.

In 1906, Bury St Edmunds celebrated the 300th anniversary of the chartering of the town as a Borough; some, if not all, of the charter was read from the steps of the Angel to an enormous crowd on Angel Hill. This roused considerable interest in the town's history and, in the following year, a great historical pageant, directed by Louis Napoleon Parker, was held in the Abbey Gardens. Since then there have been two more, one in 1959, celebrating the town's dubious connection with Magna Carta and the other in 1970, the 1100th anniversary of the martyrdom of St Edmund. If the Abbey gardens once more become an open-air theatre, is it too much to hope that, rather than another specially written script, consideration will be given to a revival of part of the N-town cycle of mystery plays?

For a long time social activities in Bury St Edmunds were concentrated into the period of the Fair, which was held at St Matthews tide, on or about 21 September. It was at this time of the year that the players of the Norwich circuit, at the end of the 18th and beginning of the 19th centuries, made their annual visit. Assemblies were also held at the Assembly House, which is now called the Athenaeum. In 1714, John Eastland, a dancing master, bought the large house which, in the hearth tax returns of 1674, had 17 hearths—no house in the town had more—and converted it into an Assembly House, for in 1715, John Hervey, first Earl of Bristol, entered in his book of expenses his subscription to Mr Eastland's New Rooms in Bury. Originally the ballroom was on the second floor, but, when the building was remodelled in 1789, the top floor was removed and a ballroom made on the ground floor as at present. The present decoration of the ballroom does not correspond with the description given in the *Bury and Norwich Post* in 1789, so it must date from a later re-furbishing; major alterations and improvements were made in 1803-1805. In the advertisements in 1789 great play was made of the fact that the building was perfectly dry and well aired, because it was of timber-framed construction rather than brick-built; on 2 July 1821 the Paving Commissioners gave permission to extend the wall on the east side of the Assembly Rooms into the street by about four inches, which may give us the date for the present brick wall on that side. Large parties from the country houses round about the town usually attended the balls held during the fair, and in connection with the Quarter Sessions and Assizes.

By the end of the 18th century, there was probably as much amusement as trade in connection with the fair. As so many people thronged the town to take advantage of the entertainments, it was well worth the while of traders who offered luxuries not normally available in a relatively small Suffolk town, to take rooms here during the fair. The advertisements in the local papers show that fashionable hairdressers, dressmakers and even a portrait painter set themselves up in the town during what was really the Bury 'season'.

When the Earl of Oxford visited the town during preparations for the fair in 1732, he noted that a bear had been stabled in the Abbey Gate, perhaps an early example of a dancing bear such as that captured in Mr Jarman's well-known photograph. It was certainly not the first unusual beast to be displayed in the town for, in 1520-21, the Keeper of the Shrine of St Edmund paid, by the order of the Prior, 2d to two men who came with a camel.

Surviving account rolls of the Sacrists of the Abbey of St Edmund show that music within the Abbey was not exclusively liturgical, for there are payments to minstrels on St Edmund's night and at Christmas. From a surviving account of the keeper of the shrine of St Edmund, it seems as though minstrels kept by distinguished visitors to the Abbey were encouraged to sing for the community, for there are payments to the minstrels of the King, the Prince and Lord Curson in the account for 1520-21.

Soon after the Corporation was set up, it became the practice to have official musicians, sometimes known as the waites, or in later times, the town musick, who nearly always provided the music at Corporation feasts. Payments to John Grene in the Feoffees' accounts suggest that he conducted the town music for several years from 1619 and, in 1622, the sum of £3 7s 0d was paid to Thomas Bright for '7 yards of blew cloth ix s. the yard for liveries for the towne wayts in the tyme when Roberte Browne was Receivior'(1621); a further sum of 54s 6d was paid to the goldsmith for silver 'cognizaunces'(badges) for the waites. When Mr Alderman Discipline was sworn as Alderman in 1729, instead of the town music, the 'high German music' from London played at the feast.

Oratorios were also popular in 18th century Bury St Edmunds and a special season was held to mark the opening of the new organ of St James's Church in September 1760. On Monday 1 September The Dettengen 'or Mr Handel's New *Te Deum*' was performed as well as his *Jubilate, Coronation Anthems,* an anthem by Dr Boyce, 'with several concertos etc.' were to be performed in the church in the morning, while in the evening, in the Assembly Rooms, 'the noble oratorio of

Joshua' was to be performed 'by desire'. On the following day, there was to be a performance of *Messiah* with a concerto on the organ, played by Mr Dupecis in the morning and, in the evening, *Acis and Galatea*, with a concerto and solos. On the Wednesday, *Judas Maccabeus* was performed in the morning and, in the evening 'the Great Oratorio of *Saul*'. The vocal parts were performed by Signora Passerini and Mrs Scott (formerly Miss Young) and by Mr Nair's boys from St James's and many others. Tickets for these concerts cost 5s each, and the doors of the church were to be open before nine in the morning, the performance to begin at ten, while the evening concerts were to begin at six o'clock precisely, and were to be followed by a ball. Assuming that Mr Nair was the organist at St James's Church here and the local choirboys were taking part, the practice of using a local chorus with distinguished visiting soloists was already established. Signora Passerini had been recommended to Handel by Telemann, and she sang in *Messiah* with his company in 1754 both at Covent Garden and at the Foundling Hospital Chapel. If, as some books state, *Messiah* was performed in Bury St Edmunds during Handel's lifetime, no evidence has been found; perhaps this performance, little more than a year after his death, is meant.

Outdoor exercise must always have included walking and, when the Earl of Oxford visited the town in September 1732, he noted that avenues of trees had been planted in the churchyard to make a pleasant promenade: they are shown on Warren's plan of 1747, along the two paths which run from near the Norman Tower, one to the Nottyngham porch of St Mary's church, and the other across the churchyard, passing the west end of the chapel of the charnel. D.E. Davy noted that the avenues were of poplars, not limes as at present. From 1831, when Nathaniel Hodson laid out the area which had once formed the great court and the garden of the Abbot's palace as a botanic garden, this became a favourite place for those who could afford either to subscribe or pay a casual entrance fee. To commemorate the Coronation of King George V in 1911, a subscription was organised to raise £650 to satisfy the lessee, and to enable everyone to enjoy the gardens free of charge; in 1953 the Borough Council acquired the freehold.

Many people still know the junction, now marked by a double roundabout, of Parkway and Cullum Road with Westgate Street and Out Westgate, as Butts Corner, a lingering reminder of an age when archery was encouraged and, at times, enforced, not only as a healthy sport but as a real contribution towards the defence of the realm. Archery was also one of the sports allowed in the early statutes of the Grammar School. In 1581 there was a dispute between the men of the town and Thomas Badby, who was then the owner of the Abbey precinct, which indicates that there were 'a paire of comon buttes for the usinge and exercysinge of shoting at which buttes all and every persone have or might have used at all tyme to exercyse shootinge' at the west end of the Vinefield either on, or very close to, the site where the School was to have its home for many years in more recent times.

In Victorian times, cricket became popular and was much enjoyed by the boys of the Grammar School, whose masters as often as not played alongside the boys. When Dr Sankey was interviewed for the post of Headmaster 1879, he saw a banner inscribed 'Vote for Sankey' carried in front of the windows of the Governors' room, for the boys believed that he was the best cricketer of the three candidates.

The coming of the railway must have enormously increased the range of places visited by sportsmen; once railway travel became the accepted means of getting about, Bury St Edmunds, like many other towns, was able to host meetings of all kinds. The Royal Show was held here from 15-19 July 1867, although the people of Ipswich had done all they could to establish their claim to the event. The showground was in Eastgate Street, near to where the by-pass now crosses the road, not far from the long-since vanished Eastgate Station, and a theatrical-looking structure was erected to house the entrances. On a more cerebral level, the Royal Archaeological Institute visited the town from 20-27 July 1869 and, in the Suffolk Record Office, there is a journal kept by one of those who attended, Wilberforce Morrell; he heard Samuel Tymms, the historian of St Mary's, read part of his work to the assembled gathering in the church 'in Feeble Tones'.

ABOVE: This drawing probably dates from c1800, but the Rising Sun in Risbygate Street has hardly altered. (St E) BELOW: The Suffolk between 1868 and 1872. The Hotel was due to close in December 1996. (OGJ)

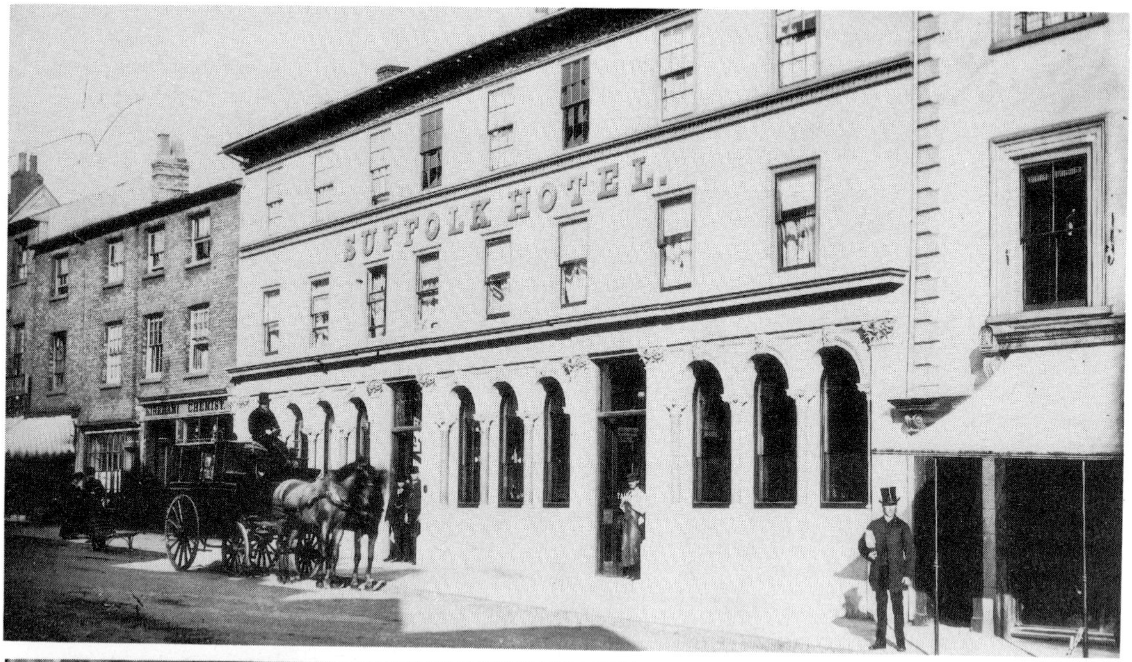
SUFFOLK HOTEL.

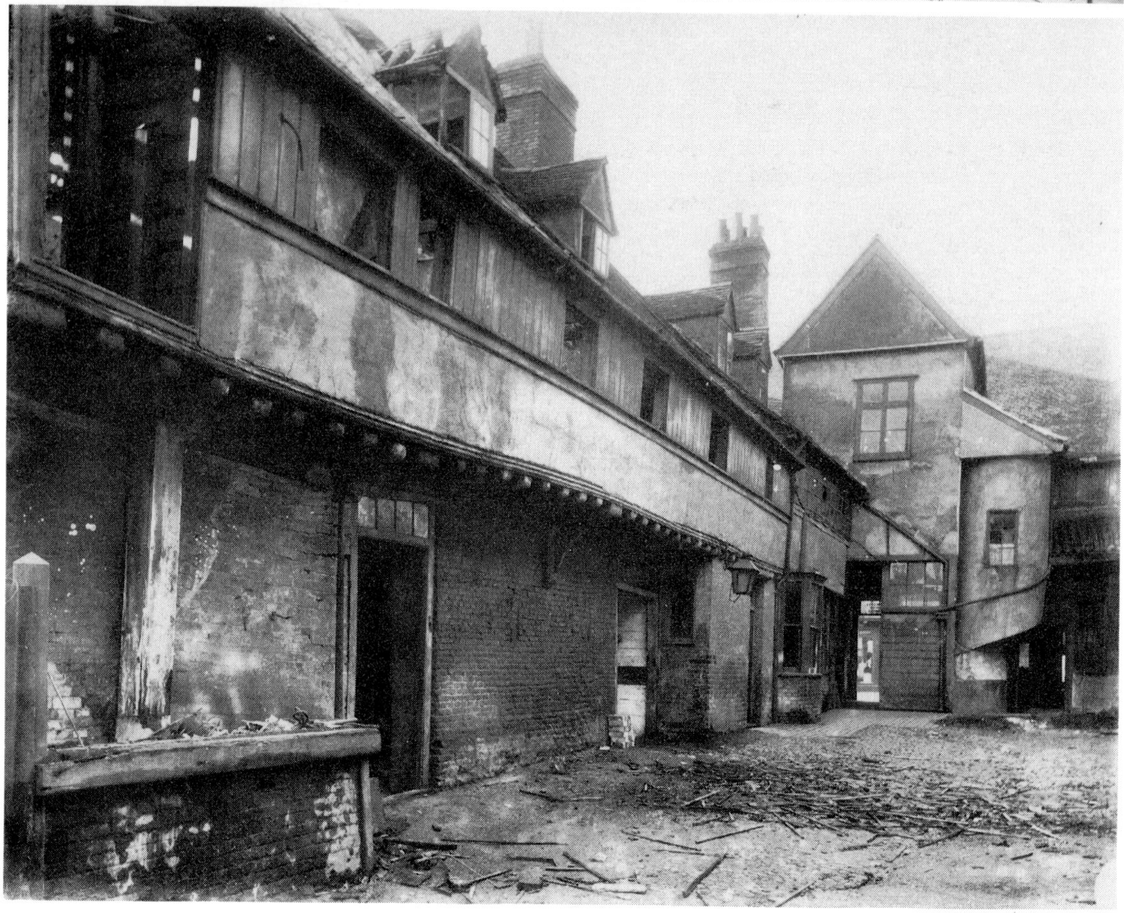

OPPOSITE ABOVE: The Suffolk later in the century, after it had been altered, when the coach entrance was blocked up. (OGJ) BELOW: The galleries of the Half Moon in the Butter Market (near W H Smith and Living) before the inn was demolished. (OGJ) ABOVE: The restored auditorium of the Theatre Royal, 1970. (OGJ) BELOW: Press Conference to launch the National Appeal for the final stage of the Theatre Royal restoration, 1964. Left to right, front row: Margaret Rawlings, Lord Euston (now Duke of Grafton), the Mayor and Mayoress, Cllr and Mrs Shearing, Michael Denison, Dulcie Gray; second row: the Duke of Grafton, Air Vice Marshal S. F. Vincent, Miss D. Pleydell Bouverie, Angus Wilson, Gwen Francgon Davis, Jevon Brandon Thomas; third row: Mrs M. Statham, Mr W. Mothersole and Miss G. Davy. (BFP)

At the THEATRE in BURY,
On Tuesday, October the Fifteenth, will be presented a COMEDY,
CALLED,

The LADY's Last STAKE:
Or, The WIFE's Resentment.

(Written by the late COLLEY CIBBER, Esq;)

Lord WRONGLOVE, Mr. D O W N I N G.
    SURGEON,   Mr.   Du-B E L L A M Y.
    BRUSH,   Mr.   S M I T H,
Lord GEORGE BRILLIANT, Mr. D E A T H.
    PORTER,   Mr.   C R O U S E.
    Stranger,   Mr.   C H A L M E R S,
  First Ruffian,   Mr.   B A N N I S T E R.
  Second Ruffian, Mr.   W E S T O N.
Sir FRIENDLY MORAL, Mr. H O L L A N D.

Lady WRONGLOVE,   Mrs. I B B O T.
Mrs. HARTSHORN, Mrs. H O L L A N D.
Lady GENTLE,   Mrs.   C H A L M E R S.
Miss NOTABLE,   Mrs. D E A T H.
Mrs. CONQUEST,   Mrs. Du-B E L L A M Y.

To which will be added a FARCE, called,

The M I N O R.

(Written by SAMUEL FOOTE, Esq;)

The PARTS of SHIFT, SMIRK, and Mrs. COLE, with the EPILOGUE
(after the Manner of the Original,) by Mr. BANNISTER.
    The   M I N O R, Mr.   S M I T H.
Sir WILLIAM WEALTHY, Mr. C H A L M E R S.
  LOADER,   Mr.   D O W N I N G.
Richard WEALTHY, Mr.   H O L L A N D.
  L U C Y,   Mrs.   W E S T O N.

BOXES, 3s.—PIT, 2s. 6d.—FIRST GALLERY, 1s. 6d. UPPER GAL. 1s.
To begin at Six o'Clock.

TICKETS to be had of Mr. GRIFFITH, at Mr. Royal's in the Whiting-Street, and of Mr. CROUSE, at Mr. Digby's in the Market-Place.

☞ Places may be taken at the Theatre from 10 to 12 each Morning.

For ONE MORNING only.

At the THEATRE in BURY,
On WEDNESDAY October the 16th. 1765.

The CELEBRATED COMIC

LECTURE
UPON
HEADS.

Consisting of THREE PARTS.

With some Additions to the ORIGINAL,

Will be EXHIBITED,

BY

Mr. Griffith.

BOXES, 3s.—PIT, 2s.—GALLERY, 1s. 6d —Upper G

To begin precisely at Twelve o'Clock.

TICKETS to be had at the Usual PL

By a Company of YOUNG GENTLEMEN.

At the ASSEMBLY-ROOM, in BURY,

On WEDNESDAY, January 7, 1784,

Will be prefented a Tragedy, called,

The Orphan of China.

(Written by MURPHY.)

Zamti,	Mafter HEIGHAM,
Hamet,	Mafter OAKES,
Timurkan,	Mafter BORTON,
Octar,	Mafter J. BORTON,
Mirvan,	Mafter J. MATHEW,
Morat,	Mafter WOODWARD,
Orafming,	Mafter H. MATHEW,
And Etan,	Mafter G. MATHEW,
Mandane, by	Mafter LAWTON.

To which will be added an Entertainment, called,

The MINOR.

Sir William Wealthy,	Mafter BORTON,
Mr. Richard Wealthy,	Mafter OAKES,
Loader,	Mafter J. BORTON,
Shift,	Mafter HEIGHAM,
Dick,	Mafter J. MATHEW,
Transfer,	Mafter WOODWARD,
And Sir George Wealthy,	Mafter G. MATHEW,
Mother Cole,	Mafter HEIGHAM,
And Lucy,	Mafter LAWTON.

Tickets to be had at ANDERSON's Coffee-Houfe, from Eleven till One on Wednefday Morning, and all other Days of Playing, at One Shilling and Sixpence each.

The Doors to be opened at Five, and fo begin precifely at Six o'Clock.——No HALF-PRICE.

☞ It will be efteemed an additional Favour, if the Company who mean to honour the Performers with their Prefence, will be punctual to their Time, as the frequent opening of the Door will otherwife hinder the Performance.

N. B. No Admittance on any Account behind the Scenes.

OPPOSITE ABOVE: The Queen Mother visits the recently restored Theatre Royal, 1968. Also in the photograph are Air Vice Marshal Stanley Vincent, Vice Chairman of the Trust which restored the theatre, Neville Blackburne, Secretary of the Management Company, Tony Budgen, Administrator, Michael Saddington, stage manager and Chris Norman, electrician.(BFP) BELOW: As well as plays, all manner of diversions were offered during the time of the Fair, often shows of those with physical deformities. Here a play and a comical lecture are advertised on the same bill, 1765.(SRO(B)) ABOVE: Play bill, *The Orphan of China*, performed by the grammar school boys for charity.(SRO(B))

ABOVE: The 1907 Pageant, the Finale. This and subsequent pageants have been held in the Abbey Gardens.(SRO(B)) BELOW: The 1959 Magna Carta Pageant: Parliament meets at Bury St Edmunds, 1447. Performers include Margaret Pettitt, Patricia Lord, Rae Pitchers, Russell Williams, Yvonne Farrow, Ralph Ambrose, Tony Tillbrook, Denise Riley, Rita Hammond, George Butcher and Norah Stavely.(SRO(B))

ABOVE: Although it was not a spa town, Bury St Edmunds nevertheless attracted a throng of fashionable people, who attended the balls and other entertainments. This caricature indicates that a Master of Ceremonies presided over the Assembly Rooms in their hey-day.(St E) BELOW: The widow's coffee house kept by Letitia Rookes in a house between the Norman Tower and St James's Church; here her daughters are looking from the upper windows. There is no evidence that it was ever a house of ill repute. From Warren's plan, 1747. RIGHT: Letitia Rookes, from a caricature, possibly by H.W. Bunbury, 1750-1811.(JK)

PART I.

Grand Sinfonia, No. 3, ... HAYDN
Glee, Miss M. Cramer, Messrs. Terrail, Horncastle, and Phillips,
    "The Rose of the Valley," . . . . Harmonized by W. KNYVETT
Scena, Miss Paton, "Softly sighs the voice of Evening," ⎱ (DER FREYSCHUTZ)
Scena, Mr. Braham, "O, I can bear my Fate no longer," ⎰   C. M. VON WEBER
Trio, Two Violoncelli and Double Bass,
    Messrs. Lindley and Anfossi . . . . CORELLI
Aria, Madame Caradori Allan,
    "Una voce poco fà," . . . . . (Il Barbiere di Siviglia) . . . . . . ROSSINI
Duet, Messrs. Braham and E. Taylor,
    "As I saw fair Clora," . . . . HAYDN
Recit. ed Aria, Miss M. Cramer,
    "Dove sono," . . . . (Figaro) . . . . MOZART
Duetto, Madame Caradori Allan and Miss Paton, Con Coro,
    "Se tu m'ami," . . . . . . (Aureliano in Palmira) . . . . ROSSINI
Ballad, Mr. Phillips, "O no we never mention her," (French Melody)
Finale to La Clemenza di Tito,
    The Solos by Mr. Braham and Mr. Horncastle . . . . MOZART

PART II.

Grand Overture to Der Freyschutz, ... C. M. VON WEBER
Recit. and Air, Mr. Horncastle "O speed my bark," . . . . BARNETT
Duetto, Madame Caradori Allan and Mr. Braham,
    "Crudel per che finora," . . . . . . (Figaro) . . . . MOZART
Aria, Mr. E. Taylor,
    "Non piu Andrai," . . . . (Figaro) . . . . MOZART
Concerto Flute, Mr. Nicholson . . . . NICHOLSON
Ballad, Miss Paton, "Jock O'Hazle dean,"
    (Accompanied by Herself on the Piano Forte)
Scena, "Alfred's Soliloquy in the Neatherd's Cot," . . . . RAUZZINI

Finale,   "GOD SAVE THE KING,"
            Verse, by the Principal Singers, and Chorus.

LEFT: Wild animals have long been popular; a Russian bear in the Butter Market, c1907.(OGJ) RIGHT: The programme for the first concert of the Musical Festival held at St Mary's in 1828.(SRO(B)) BELOW: Bury Grammar School Cricket team, 1874; left to right: Dewing, Flegg, Fitch, Perkins, Gooch, Kidson, Bent, Rev George Herbert Statham MA, Quick; in front, King and Cobbold. OPPOSITE ABOVE: Appeal for funds to enable the Abbey Gardens to become a public park. £200 of the £650 required was given by the then MP, Col Walter Guinness, who later became Lord Moyne of Bury St Edmunds. The gardens were leased by the Council until 1953, when it acquired the freehold.(SRO(B)) BELOW: Round Tablers about to leave for their hand-over dinner at the House of Commons, 1959. Those in the picture include D. Raphael, M.B. Hales, D.W. Frost, D.J. Evans, L.C.J. Sewell, D. Clark, V. Brega, [Sir]Graham McMillan, incoming Chairman, M.D. Fulcher, M.P. Statham, outgoing Chairman, C. Dennis, A. Cuffley, A. Kenyon, D.J. Pitchers, A. Sneezum, M. Osborn, R. Land, L. Davidson and L. Glasswell.

Sir (or Madam),

With a view of commemorating the auspicious event of the Coronation of King George V., it has been suggested that a **Public Park** be provided for the inhabitants of Bury St. Edmund's and the neighbourhood.

The site suggested is the Abbey Gardens.

These grounds, which comprise an area of over 13 Acres, situated in the centre of the town, are too well known to necessitate a detailed description.

It will be remembered that this was the site of the St. Edmundsbury Pageant in 1907, and it was felt at that time by all who took part in that ceremonial or visited the same, that some steps should be taken to acquire these grounds for the public, and also to endeavour to preserve those ancient ruins which so fully deserve the veneration of all who are interested in the historical past of our ancient and Royal Borough.

Having this idea in view, in order to take the gardens over from the present tenant, we beg to enlist your sympathies in this movement, and respectfully solicit a promise of a contribution towards the purchase-money which it will be necessary to raise, in the event of the scheme being adopted by the Town Council.

An independent valuation has been made, and the sum ultimately agreed upon by the Lessee amounts to £650.

We are endeavouring to obtain promises of financial support to that extent, and should the required amount be forthcoming, it is earnestly hoped that the Corporation will see their way clear to take the gardens over and maintain them.

OWEN ALY CLARK, } Aldermen.
T. H. NICE,

ABOVE: Round Table in the late 1950s organised Whit Monday Fetes to raise money to buy and run a coach to enable people to visit patients at Newmarket General Hospital and St Audreys Hospital, Melton. Launching the 'sputnik', 1958. BELOW: The Abbey ruins from the old Botanic Garden, 1821; the bridge also appears in Quinton's water colour of the Abbey ruins.(JK)

Lessons Learnt

Two mediaeval schools in Bury St Edmunds had, by the 1260s, given their name to Schoolhall Street, which has now become Honey Hill and part of Raingate Street. The mediaeval grammar school stood on the site of Shire Hall, and Abbot Samson himself was at one time, before he became a monk, the Master of the school at Bury St Edmunds, although he himself had received his early education at Diss before going to the schools at Paris. Samson endowed the school with three marks a year out of the church at Wetherden, to ensure that the schoolmaster had a regular source of income, and he built stone houses to ensure that in future the 40 scholars might be free from paying fees. The schoolmaster and his pupils were the only people in the town who were not subject to the Sacrist; the Abbot alone had jurisdiction over the schoolmaster, who himself had the special privilege of jurisdiction over his scholars. As bequests to pay the fees of clerks studying at the University were frequently made in the late mediaeval period, the school was presumably capable of producing scholars fitted to go on to the University.

The song-school was controlled by the Dussegild, which was of early origin and had many privileges granted to it by Abbot Baldwin; according to one account it was a re-formation by Baldwin of the seculars who had cared for St Edmund's shrine before Cnut founded the Benedictine house at Bury St Edmunds, and he established them in the Church of St Denis, which he had set up as a parish church, and which Anselm replaced with the first church of St James. However, according to notes on the Suffolk Guild Certificates of 1389, it then consisted of a master and twelve clerks in St Mary's Church. The objects of the guild were to chant at the funerals of Bury monks; their possessions were eight acres in Melford and five shops and a cottage in Bury St Edmunds. Nothing is said about the school, but there is abundant evidence that the members of the Dussegild appointed the master and chose the scholars of the song-school, and they jealously forbade anyone to teach the singing of psalms and canticles without their licence. The position of the song-school is known with certainty, for the Sacrist's rental of 1433 makes it clear that it abutted on the east end of St Mary's Church.

At the dissolution of the Abbey, the monastic grammar school was closed down and, some ten years later, when the chantries and guilds were suppressed, the chantry certificate for Bury St Edmunds contains the well-known plea for some of their endowments to be used to replace some of the things which the townspeople had lost at the dissolution, such as a school and a hospital; it pointed out that there were more than 3,000 'howseling people', or communicants, in the town, besides many children, indicating a total population of rather more than 4,500. It was not, however, until 1550 that King Edward VI founded a grammar school which still continues as the King Edward VI School, now a co-educational Upper School.

The first school hall (as the buildings were called until the 1970s) under the new foundation was the former Guildhall of the guild of St Thomas à Becket in Eastgate Street, which may well have been the buildings now called the Ancient House and the Old Guildhall. This building is of the right period, and the abuttals given when the Governors sold the property in 1665 seem consistent with a building on this site. From Eastgate Street, the school moved in 1665 to Northgate Street, where the school house, now known as St Michael's Close, has altered little over the years, save that the Roman cement, with which the old brick-work was covered in 1811 and which the *Bury and Norwich Post* considered to be 'the best imitation of Portland stone we ever witnessed', has recently been removed. In time the Northgate Street building became dilapidated and inconvenient, and in 1883 the school moved into new buildings, designed by Sir Arthur Blomfield, in the former vineyard of the Abbey, some of which are now St James' Middle School, while the former boarding house has recently been converted into luxury flats, which must have some of the finest views in the town.

Many distinguished men were educated at Bury School, as it was usually known. Sir Simonds D'Ewes, whose autobiography is full of information about the proceedings of Parliament during the years 1640-48, when he was member for Sudbury, was educated there. John and Forth, two of the sons of John Winthrop, the first Governor of Massachusetts, were also educated there, and John (a graduate of Trinity College, Dublin, who was elected a Fellow of the Royal Society in 1663) was to become the first Governor of Connecticut. A surviving letter from Forth when a schoolboy at Bury, to his brother, then at Trinity College, Dublin, confirms what can be guessed from the evidence of the parish registers, that there was much illness in Bury St Edmunds in 1623, when virtually famine conditions ensured that life was hard and precarious for all classes. One old boy of the school, Archbishop Sancroft, was tried as one of the seven bishops who refused to take the oath of allegiance to William and Mary, and the Judge who heard the case was another, Robert Wright, the Lord Chief Justice. The first person to attempt to write the history of Bury St Edmunds, John Batteley (1646-1708), Archdeacon of Canterbury, was also educated at Bury School; his work, which only covers the period up to 1272, is written in Latin and was posthumously published in 1745, Sir James Burrough having helped with the illustrations. Sir James Burrough (1691-1764), Master of Gonville and Caius College, Cambridge, for the last ten years of his life, was both a distinguished antiquary and a well-known amateur architect. He advised Elizabeth Felton, second wife of the first Earl of Bristol, when she built herself a splendid house on the site of the family's old house in Honey Hill and, at his death, left his collection of materials for the history of Bury St Edmunds to the library of St James's Church. One volume survives to this day and is still worth consulting, especially for notes and correspondence about events in his lifetime—when the foundations of the Provost's house were being dug in the 1730s, Burrough saw and recorded the buttresses of the nave wall of the Abbey church. Another former pupil, Bishop Blomfield, was one of the leading figures in the Church of England in the 19th century and had much to do with the establishment of the Ecclesiastical, now the Church, Commissioners; as Bishop of London, he also did a great deal to promote church building in newly developing areas of that City.

The school has an extensive archive, which includes a great deal of material of value to the student of the history of education, including early inventories of the books and other equipment used in the school, as well as the statutes under which the school was run at various periods. The first statutes of 1550, which are in Latin, at some time strayed from the main body of the school records and are now in the British Museum; then the school day lasted from six in the morning until five in the evening, with a break for dinner from eleven until one, and all had to provide themselves with ink, paper, a penknife, pens and books, using their knees as a table when they had to write. The books they studied, apart from the Book of Common Prayer, were in Latin or Greek, additions to the curriculum being added slowly. One of the headmasters, Edward Leedes, who was in charge of the school from 1663-1707, published a book of sentences for the boys to translate from English into Latin, which give some glimpses of life in Bury St Edmunds at the time. Most of the old and valuable books from the Grammar School library, which was established when the School was founded in 1550, were deposited in the Cambridge University Library in 1971. Its greatest treasure is a Psalter which once belonged to the Abbey of St Edmund.

For a considerable period the Governors of the Grammar School ran a poor boys' school in, or at least on the site of, buildings which were originally the chapel of St John-at-Hill in the churchyard, between the Norman Tower and St Mary's Church. This the Governors seem to have bought in about 1626, and it was adapted for use as the poor boys' school then or shortly afterwards as, in the school accounts for 1630, the Haberdon estate first appeared in the rental, with a note that it had been purchased for the poor school, no doubt as an endowment for it. References to this school are infrequent and it is not quite clear how it was organised; it seems that, in addition to teaching some poor boys—in 1696 it was four from each parish—the master had some fee paying pupils as well.

Private schools must have abounded in the town. Before the College in the street of that name became the workhouse for the incorporated parishes, a Mr Wood ran a young ladies' boarding school there, and several advertisements are to be found in the *Suffolk Mercury*. On 7 October 1723, Mr Wood announced that he had made an arrangement with Mr Eastland, the proprietor of the Assembly House then living in Norwich, by which Mr Wood was to use the 'Great Room in his (Mr Eastland's) late Dwelling House, on the Angel Hill in Bury aforesaid, call'd the Coffee Room, to teach the Schollars of him the said Mr Wood to Dance in, and to hold and keep Publicks and Balls'. Mr Wood was to continue with his school in the College, and Mr Eastland was to continue to hold his Assemblies 'monthly and at other times of the year as usual'. Later, Mr Eastland and Mr Wood must have been in competition, for on 24 January 1725 *The Suffolk Mercury* gave the rates 'of Mr Eastland's Boarding School on the Angel Hill in St Edmunds Bury, Suffolk; for plain Work, and all Sorts of Work done with a Needle, or without, and Boarding, 14l. a Year, Dancing 10s Entrance, and 10s per Quarter, Writing, including Pens, Ink and Paper, 10s per Quarter. The French Tongue is also taught very reasonably. Musick is also taught, at very reasonable Rates'.

Charles Blomfield, the father of the Bishop, kept his private school in a house on the north-east corner of Lower Baxter Street and Looms Lane; the health centre which now stands on the site is called Blomfield House. An earlier school in Lower Baxter Street was run by a Mr Crew, several of whose former pupils gave evidence in 1721 when there was an enquiry into a supposed right-of-way from Lower Baxter Street to Angel Hill.

The 'central schools' established by the Suffolk Society for the Education of the Poor in the Principles of the Established Church (SPCK), in 1819 educated 157 boys and 80 girls, and there were over 20 boys who also attended as Sunday scholars. In the Record Office there is a log book relating to this school between 1822 and 1827, which is shown on Lenny's map of 1823 as the National School in Field (now Kings) Road, opposite the *Free Press* offices. It was run by visitors, who included the town clergy and other prominent townsmen. Boys aged between five and 10 years of age were admitted, mainly from the town, but a few from the surrounding parishes, and were required to attend church on Sunday as well as attending school during the week, the average attendance for each month usually being between 200 and 220. Each year, as soon as harvesting began, the school closed for about a month. Parental involvement was considerable, as parents were required to meet the visitors when the boys entered and left the school, and in all cases of serious truancy or other misbehaviour. There was a 'Reward Box', from which Bibles, Prayer Books or other devotional works were bought for the boys, either as they made their way through the school or on leaving. Some boys, whose conduct seems to have been above-average, also received a money payment when they withdrew from the school.

The *Bury Guide Book* of 1821 indicated that there were then three charity schools which educated 40 boys in one case and 50 girls in the two others. These schools, founded in 1707, had a settled fund of £70 *per annum* and the children were all clothed and taught the English language. The children of non-conformists were provided for at the Lancasterian School in College Street, which had been founded in 1811, and to which about 200 were admitted.

When the Charity Commissioners drew up a scheme for the funds of the Guildhall Feoffees in 1842, a part of their income was set aside to provide schools. These schools, and the Grammar School, ensured that Bury St Edmunds offered far better educational opportunities than were available in many places, but it seems that neither the Grammar School nor the Guildhall Feoffees' Commercial School received the support from the town which might have been expected; both tended to have fewer pupils than they could have taken. Whereas the Grammar School was always associated with the Church of England, the Feoffment Schools were open to children of any denomination. The Commercial School offered a sound education to boys not intending to go on to the University, in all probability better than that to be had at the Grammar School, which for a long time had a curriculum confined to the classics. The Feoffees had the report of HM Inspector of 1846 printed, from which it appears that Mr Craske, the Master, was an exceptional teacher.

In the course of the 19th century, schools were established in connection with the three Anglican Parish Churches and with St Edmunds Roman Catholic Church.

Elementary education in the town was re-organised in the 1930s, when the Borough Education Committee set about the replacement of old and inadequate buildings, in a scheme which saw the demolition of the old Risbygate Schools and their replacement with St Edmundsbury and the Silver Jubilee Schools in Grove Road. The Silver Jubilee School, so called to mark the Silver Jubilee of King George V and Queen Mary in 1935, was opened in 1936 and provided education for the older children who did not go to a grammar school, while St Edmundsbury School, which celebrated its own golden jubilee in 1987, took in the younger children from the former St James's School. Grammar school education for girls as well as boys had been afforded by the County School in Northgate Street, which was established under the 1902 Act. In 1947, Bury St Edmunds ceased to be an education authority, and the West Suffolk Education Committee became responsible for all maintained schools in the town. The Grammar School was then merged into the state system.

A significant part of the self-help movement in education in the town is associated with the Athenaeum, which was formed by an amalgamation of the Archaeological and Young Men's Institutes and had its home in Guildhall Street for a time, until in 1854 it bought the Assembly Rooms, which have now taken its name. Many of the great names of Victorian England— Dickens, Thackeray and the astronomer Sir George Airy (whose lecture inspired the purchase of the telescope on the roof of the Athenaeum) are just a few examples — lectured to the organisation on all sorts of subjects, and its members had at their disposal a library and reading room. These lectures were without doubt the forerunners of the adult education movement of today.

OPPOSITE: The Ancient House, Eastgate Street, which may well have been the first home of the Grammar School when it was founded in 1550.(SRO(B)) ABOVE: The former Grammar School building in Northgate Street (St Michael's Close), 1747. BELOW: The Northgate Street building after it was enlarged in 1762 to provide accommodation for 30 borders. A late 19th century view.(OGJ)

Fundamental and standing Rules and Orders

FOR THE

CHARITY-SCHOOLS in St. EDMUND's BURY in SUFFOLK.

WHEREAS several Schools have been lately set up and established, by the voluntary Subscriptions of charitable and well-dispos'd Persons in the several Parishes of this Town, for instructing poor Children, whose Parents are not able to afford them Education, and for qualifying them to get their Living; and forasmuch as good Government necessarily conduces to those Ends, the following Rules and Orders are by the said Subscribers directed and appointed to be observed.

That there be a general Meeting four times in the Year at the most usual Quarterly Feasts; viz. *Lady, Midsummer, Michaelmas,* and *Christmas*; and that *Thursday* before Quarter-Day, immediately after Prayers at Church in the Afternoon, be the known Time of such general Meeting at the Council-Chamber in *Guild-Hall*.

That the Boys elected into the Schools, shall have green Caps and Neckcloths, and the Girls Dolphins, with green Worsted or Taffaty.

That Eleven Persons be chosen, at the general Meetings before *Christmas* and *Midsummer*, out of the Subscribers, who are to have the Denomination of Stewards, and to give all necessary Orders and Directions, as they shall think fit, in relation to the said Schools, between the said general Meetings, and that five of them have Power to act; and if there be an even Number, the Chairman is to have a double Voice; which Chairman is to be chosen at every such Meeting by the Stewards then present.

That the Alderman and preaching Ministers for the Time being, if Subscribers, be always of the Number of Stewards.

That there be a Receiver annually chosen, at a Quarterly Meeting, who shall keep a fair Account of all Receipts and Disbursements, ready for the View of all the Contributers or others, who may have Reason,

the Morning, and from One to Five in the Evening, from the 10th of *February*, to the 10th of *October*: And from Eight to Eleven in the Morning, and from One to Four in the Evening; the rest of the Year, *Saturdays* only excepted, when they are constantly throughout the Year to break up School at Four in the Afternoon.

That they take particular Care of the Manners and Behaviour of the poor Children; and, by all proper Methods, that they discourage and punish the Beginnings of Vice, and particularly Lying, Swearing, Cursing, taking God's Name in vain, and Profanation of the Lord's Day.

That they set a good Example themselves, by a constant and regular frequenting the Publick Worship and Sacraments; and that the Children, on all Opportunities, be brought to the Publick Prayers at the Beginning of Divine Service, and behave themselves with due Reverence; but particularly on *Sundays* and Holy-Days.

That they call over the Names of all the Children, every Morning and Afternoon, to know whether they come constantly at School-Hours; and if any be missing, to mark their Names with a Note for tardy, and another for absent, in Bills to be laid before the Stewards, in order to their Correction or Expulsion.

That they suffer not the Children to break up above three Times in the Year, namely on the Eve of the three usual Festivals; and so by no Means at *Bury*-Fair, beginning on the Festival of St. *Matthew*.

That except on some particular Occasion, to be approv'd by the Stewards for the Time being, *Thursdays* in the Afternoon be the only Time allow'd to the Master and Mistresses to grant an occasional Recess for the Children to play, which they are by no Means to grant too frequently, but never when more than one Festival shall happen in the same Week.

AN
HYMN,
TO BE SUNG BY
The Charity Children of Bury St. Edmund's,
On SUNDAY, OCTOBER 17, 1819,
AFTER
A SERMON,
TO BE PREACHED FOR THEIR BENEFIT,
AT ST. MARY'S CHURCH IN THE MORNING,
AND AT
ST. JAMES'S IN THE AFTERNOON,
By the Rev. C. J. BLOMFIELD, B. D.
RECTOR OF CHESTERFORD AND TUDDENHAM,
And DOMESTIC CHAPLAIN to the RIGHT REVEREND the LORD BISHOP of LONDON.

LOUD let the grateful Notes of Praise
Th' Almighty's Love proclaim;
High as his Throne our Voices raise,
To glorify his Name.

Thy Wisdom form'd us from the Dust,
Thy Mercy spares us still;
Lord in thy Pow'r alone we trust,
To guard from future Ill.

And now, while bount'ous Hands impart
The pitying Aid we need,
Thy kindred Spirit warms the Heart,
And prompts the gen'rous Deed.

Oh! while our grateful Tongues resound
Thy Praise from Earth to Heaven,
Bless thou the Hand that pours around
Those Blessings thou hast given.

And when the last, the awful close,
Shall wake the slumb'ring Dead;
Lord in thy Mercy think of those,
Who here thy Bounties spread.

AMEN.

BURY: PRINTED BY J. RACKHAM, ANGEL HILL.

OPPOSITE ABOVE: The Grammar School from the Vinefield Gate, c1945.(RWE/RH) BELOW: Some of the rules of the Charity School, 1707.(SRO(I)) LEFT: Services at which this hymn was to be sung were no doubt a money-raising effort in aid of the schools.(SRO(B)) RIGHT: Artist's impression of the Guildhall Feoffment Boys' School hall, 1843. It is little changed today.(SRO(B))

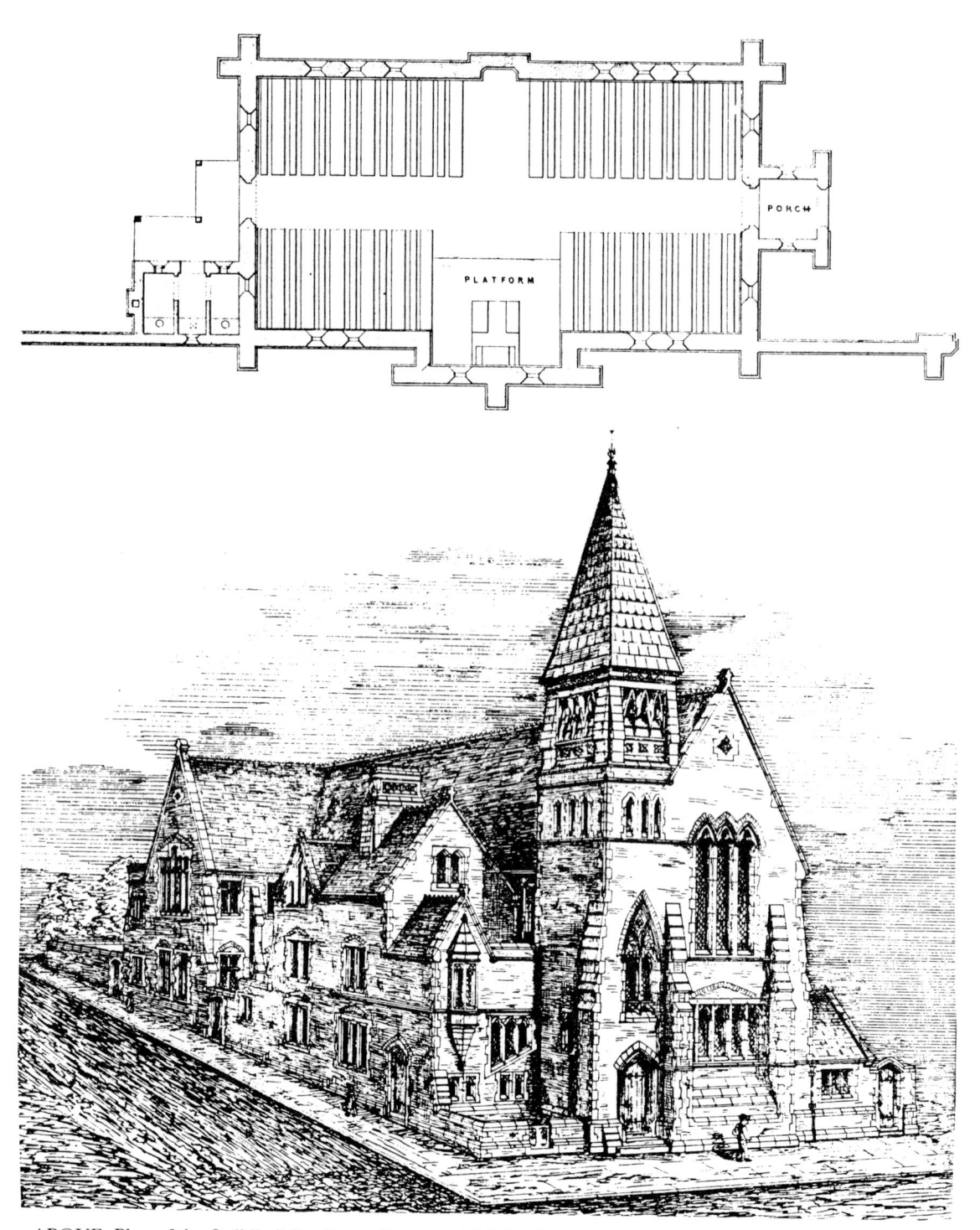

ABOVE: Plan of the Guildhall Feoffment Commercial School, 1843. Although all the boys were taught in one room, the teacher's voice could be heard in all parts and he could see all the boys' faces.(SRO(B)) BELOW: St James's National Schools, Risbygate Street, were built to the designs of Barry of Liverpool in 1846 and closed in 1937, when St Edmundsbury School opened in Grove Road. It stood where the car park on the corner of Nelson Road is now.(SRO(B))

ABOVE: Blomfield House, birthplace of Bishop Blomfield, where his father kept a preparatory school. When the house was demolished to make way for the health centre, which retains the old name, the door case was moved to a house in Bridewell Lane.(OGJ) BELOW: The Guildhall banqueting room as the reading room of the Bury and West Suffolk Library, c1890.(OGJ)

ABOVE: The Manor House, built by Elizabeth Felton, second wife of the first Earl of Bristol, was used for entertaining during Bury Fair and at other times. This photograph was probably taken early in this century when it was the home of Col Guinness, later Lord Moyne.(OGJ) BELOW: Hatter Street corner before it was burnt down in 1882.(OGJ)

In Our Own Time

Since the end of the war, Bury St Edmunds has seen a period of expansion which can only be paralleled by the twenty years between the Norman Conquest in 1066 and the compilation of Domesday Book in 1086.

Development of the additional land acquired under the West Suffolk Review Order of 1934 began slowly and, as late as 1960, momentum was only just building up. The Mildenhall Road estate was well under way and a school had been opened in 1950; there had been a little development immediately to the west of the old boundary in roads such as Minden Drive and Gainsborough Road.

When Bury St Edmunds became one of several West Suffolk towns to invite London and other firms to come here under a town expansion scheme, there were rapid changes; an agreement was made with the GLC, and houses and factories were built. The site acquired to the west of the town for a civic airport in the 1930s was used for the Western Industrial Estate and its associated housing, and was soon followed by the Howard estate and then the Nowton Road housing. The rapid increase in population is best shown in the population table (Appendix 1). The decision by the Department of the Environment, after a public enquiry, to allow building on the hill east of the town is regarded by many as an aesthetic disaster; it looks like 'toy-town' from the author's study window. Street names reflecting aspects of the town's history seem, in theory, a good idea, but in practice do little to help people to find their way about.

Industrial estates were also built, and the firms who have come to the town in recent years have revolutionised its economic life. Gone are the days when the economy of the town was firmly rooted in agriculture, and businesses of many kinds have been introduced; Barber Greene Olding, who made road making machinery, Nilfisk, the Danish vacuum cleaner manufacturers; Vitality Bulbs and Vintens, who make specialised cameras all now take their place alongside Greene King and the sugar beet factory. Many small specialist businesses are now settled here too, such as Garner Wilson who makes violin bows.

The market was being developed in the early 1960s, when buildings for the new pig market were put up. Nowadays, it seems incredible to think that it was then usual for cattle and sheep to be driven to market on Wednesdays, adding to the already heavy traffic in Risbygate Street. The cattle and provision markets remain an important feature in the economy of the town, and the tolls collected by the Borough Council are an important source of revenue. At the time of writing, a proposal to remove the Cattle Market from the St Andrews Street/Risbygate Street site is under consideration

Local Government Re-organisation in 1974 saw West Suffolk merged into a single county of Suffolk, with its administrative headquarters in Ipswich. The Borough of Bury St Edmunds disappeared too, to be replaced by the newly created Borough of St Edmundsbury, which included the former Thingoe and Clare Rural District Councils, and the Haverhill Urban District Council areas, as well as Bury St Edmunds itself. There may be less interest in local council affairs now than there was in the days of the Borough of Bury St Edmunds; where are the crowds which used to gather on Angel Hill to hear the local election results? Bigger is not necessarily better, and perhaps more thought should be given to adapting the traditions of an ancient borough, for a much larger area can never hope to have the same sense of community that is found in a town. A Public Relations Officer is to be appointed who will, no doubt, ensure that members of the public are better informed about matters concerning the community as a whole than has been the case.

Many new schools were built to meet the needs of people living on the new estates, and the whole system of education in the town was re-organised in 1971, when the three-tier system of first, middle and upper schools was introduced. The Grammar School, now known as King Edward VI School, the County School for Girls and St Benedict's RC Secondary Modern School all became co-educational Upper Schools for children of 13+, but King Edward's School left the old Grammar School buildings on the Vinefield for the buildings which had formerly housed the Silver Jubilee Secondary Modern School in Grove Road. Middle Schools were built on the Westley Estate, Horringer Court, and at Hardwick, while the former Grammar School buildings became St James' C of E Middle School and the Convent of St Louis became a RC Middle School, the remaining schools becoming first schools, apart from a few of the older ones which have been sold for other uses. In 1960, the West Suffolk College of Further Education (which grew out of the old Technical Institute, which had long provided evening classes) was opened, and was able to offer day-release and full-time courses, as well as an ever-increasing variety of vocational and other evening courses.

The new Police Station was opened in Raingate Street as part of the County building complex in 1964 and the new fire station was opened by HRH the Duke of Gloucester in September 1987. The Borough Council has recently acquired the former Barber Greene Factory in Western Way as its main office centre and depôt, providing space for departments formerly working from the Corporation yard near the Cattle Market. At the time of writing, the Borough Offices on Angel Hill are being modernised, so that the Council will continue to have a presence in the town centre. A Tourist Information Centre, open all the year round, was established at 6, Angel Hill, next door to the Borough Offices, in April 1987.

The former County Library Headquarters in Raingate Street became the Bury St Edmunds Branch of the Suffolk Record Office at Local Government Reorganisation and, until 1983, readers from town and the surrounding villages used the old Borough Library on Cornhill. This was replaced by the purpose-built Central Library in Sergeant's Walk, off St Andrews Street. The town still has no permanent art gallery, but the Market Cross was adapted as an exhibition room, which is called the Art Gallery, in 1972. Plans are now being prepared for an exciting new museum, based on the Manor House, which will afford space for the Borough's own art collection. The purpose-built Sports Centre was burned down in 1980 but arose, phoenix-like, in 1981, while the Nowton Court Park, which has recently been acquired by the Council, will afford extensive facilities for recreation. The Rollerbury roller skating centre is much appreciated by the young.

Thirty years ago there were no long distance 'bus services like those which nowadays link the town with London and many other parts of the country, but many trains stopped at intermediate stations between here and Ipswich and Cambridge, which augmented country 'bus services. For those without a car, travel to the surrounding villages is now far from easy. The recent closure of the 'bus station has denied passengers facilities such as waiting rooms, and must surely soon be replaced by a new 'bus inter-change.

However, if public transport leaves a great deal to be desired, the dualling of the A45 in the 1970s has improved road communications with the rest of the country in an amazing way, and must be considered one of the major events in the history of the town. Sadly, because the by-pass takes motorists through the most unpleasant parts of the town, more and more people are jumping to the quite erroneous conclusion that Bury St Edmunds is a horrid, industrial town, which could drive potential visitors - and residents - elsewhere, if the impression is not rectified.

In 1960 or thereabouts, the town had three cinemas and no theatre; now, there is only one cinema, but the Regency Theatre Royal has been restored and re-opened. The closure of the Playhouse Cinema denied the local amateur dramatic societies a stage for their performances, and was a major impetus in restoring the Theatre Royal, which had been used by Greene King as a barrel store since it closed in 1926. Amid prophecies of imminent failure, it re-opened on 1 April 1965, and is still flourishing and well repaying all the effort of a great many people involved in its restoration.

In addition to thriving amateur dramatic societies, the town caters for those with musical tastes of all kinds, from the Bach Society with its large-scale performances with professional soloists, to the chamber music club which provides an opportunity for amateur musicians to play together in small groups. There are a great number of clubs and societies catering for all manner of interests, and any issue of the *The Bury Free Press* shows how hobbies and recreations are often made the means of fund-raising for good causes.

The old West Suffolk Hospital buildings were replaced by a purpose-built district hospital in Hardwick Lane in 1973, and since then the St Edmunds Nursing Home has opened in the former Square House Hotel in St Mary's Square. New buildings have been built for clinics and operating theatres, but the old house is now one of a growing number in the town which provide long-term care for the elderly. St Nicholas Hospice was opened last year in another of Bury's good Georgian houses, Turret Close, in Westgate Street. Many people of retirement age are attracted to the town, and a high proportion of elderly residents is reflected in the provision for them both by the local authority and private enterprise.

Two new Anglican churches have been built since the war to provide for those living on the new estates north and west of the town, and it is anticipated that a third parish will be created at Moreton Hall. The development of the Nowton Road area has given rise to an ecumenical experiment, the Southgate Centre, sponsored by the Bury Council of Churches, which may well point the way for the future. In 1960, a new porch and part of a proposed cloister and in 1970, the new quire, were dedicated as the first two phases of a scheme to enlarge the Parish Church of St James to enable it to fulfil its role as the Cathedral Church of the Diocese. Work on a third stage, which will provide vestries and rooms for the choir, to replace temporary buildings which have outlived their usefulness, should begin in 1988.

Sadly, the development of the sixties and seventies has added no outstanding 20th century examples to Bury's splendid heritage of good buildings. Perhaps architects are unwilling to accept the challenge of blending modern work with that of older generations, or the planners consider that neo-Georgian is safe. One of Bury's great needs is a building of the 1980s which nevertheless respects its older neighbours.

Conflict between pedestrians and motorists in narrow streets, made even narrower when, at the end of the 17th and the beginning of the 18th centuries, permission was given for householders to build the ground floor of their houses flush with the projecting upper storeys, has still to be resolved.

The recent trend towards out-of-town shopping should not be allowed to destroy the town centre's role as a shopping area. Thirty years ago, when most people's ambition was to live outside the town, there were at least five grocers' shops in Abbeygate Street. Now, with the trend for people to move back into the town centre, there is only one.

Constant vigilance will be required to ensure that what is most worth conserving of Bury's rich inheritance is not devoured in the name of development. It is alarming in the extreme that a town with so much that is of historical and architectural importance is only now getting its first history, and at that a thumb-nail sketch. Much more detailed work is already overdue, and it can only be a matter of time before more buildings of importance disappear without any record, because no one has any idea of their importance. Almoners Barns Farm and the College are but two which have already gone; an application to demolish Eastgate Barns Farm, which is on the site, if not incorporating part of, the complex which was the headquarters of the Cellarer's estate, was deferred during October 1987. There is an enormous amount of work still to be done on the history of the town, and it could easily come too late to save the loss of important features.

If this book helps to dispel some of the romantic 'merrie England' notions about the town's history, and to make people realise that, in the past, life was not all knights in shining armour and fair ladies, monks and bishops but, for all but a very few, hard and uncomfortable, and that hard work and effort have been what really counts, it will have fulfilled its aim. It is surely time that Bury St Edmunds is known, not so much as the birthplace of Magna Carta, but as the home of Abbot Ale.

ABOVE: George Thompson's bill head.(JK) BELOW: Fire damage in 1882. This fire was started deliberately in an attempt to obtain the insurance money.(OGJ)

ABOVE: When this block of property was rebuilt, the street line was moved to widen the street at this point. In 1954, when this photograph was taken, the building on the corner was still the County Club. (OGJ)
BELOW: These cottages in Honey Hill were demolished soon after this photograph was taken in 1958. A few years ago, two houses were built on the site, and the building to their left converted into a dwelling. (OGJ)

ABOVE: This photograph of the Cornhill was taken between January 1878 and June 1880 and none of the buildings have survived. Burtons, Martin's (formerly Boots) and the Post Office are now on the site.(OGJ) BELOW: Hunter and Oliver left this shop on Cornhill c1963. Later, when Boots' new shop was built, the old shop window was retained.(OGJ) OPPOSITE ABOVE: The new Mothercare store has been built on the site of the King's Head on the corner of St Johns Street, photographed here in 1921.(OGJ) BELOW: Mustow Street at the turn of the century, before the old houses were demolished in 1926 to facilitate street widening.(OGJ)

133

LEFT: This house in Eastgate Street was built with oak salvaged from the houses demolished in Mustow Street.(OGJ) RIGHT: There is a love hate relationship with this sign on Angel Hill, often called the 'Pillar of Salt'. Motor traffic made it essential, and the Council went to great lengths to find something worthy of the site. They were advised by Mr Basil Oliver, and it was approved by the Ministry of Transport in June 1935, subject to the letters being 5" high.(HS) BELOW: This photograph of the corner of St Andrews Street and Westgate Street was taken by Oswald Jarman, aged 12, in 1921 - his first photograph, and he won £1 0s 0d with it in a junior photographic competition. Hell-fire corner was a common name for it in the '60s, when it became a notorious traffic problem. Most of the old houses have been demolished to improve the corner.(OGJ)

134

LEFT: Post-war reconstruction: building a house on the Mildenhall Road estate, c1948.(SRO(B)) BELOW: An unusual view of part of the north side of Abbeygate Street, taken from the site of the 1882 fire. Apart from the shop fronts, there have been few changes to these buildings externally.(OGJ) RIGHT: Grooms shop, with Jarman's (then Spanton's) the photographers on the left and Fenton's antique shop on the right. Traditionally, Abbeygate Street attracted high class shops often selling luxury goods, but in recent years building societies have tended to move in.(OGJ)

ABOVE: The Griffin, c1898, before it had its 'Georgian' door on the corner.(SRO(B)) BELOW: Abbeygate Street in 1952, with the road up, for removal of the wooden blocks. Many shop fronts have been altered, but above ground-floor level, much remains unchanged.(OGJ)

LEFT: Cupola House in the 1890s. Alterations have been made to the ground floor doors and windows and tiles applied to the gable end.(OGJ)
RIGHT: The Misses Wing lived at this house from about 1874 until 1885 or after. It is little changed.(OGJ) BELOW: Abbeygate Street, perhaps c1955. The horse pulling the milk float was apt to bite.(OGJ)

137

ABOVE: Whiting Street about 1950. The building with the baker's shop and the Hovis sign has been demolished and replaced by a modern one.(OGJ) BELOW: With an increasingly elderly population, housing for those who are unable to care for themselves has been provided both by the Council and by private enterprise in recent years. Cllr Mrs Barbara Jennings (now Hill) opens Beeton's Lodge, 1983. Also in the photograph are Ald A.F.S. Davies, Mr D. Green, the Housing Manager and Mrs Geraldine Jennings, the Mayoress.(BJH)

The second state of Kendall's print of Angel Hill, 1774, which shows the Angel rebuilt, the Assembly Rooms (now the Athenaeum) with three storeys. The Borough Offices stand on the site of the early 18th century house on the right, but were built back from the original road line. At the house next door, shown here with three gables, there lived at various times Poley Clopton, who founded Clopton's Hospital, and Edward Crisp, the victim of Arundel Coke's assassination attempt.(OGJ)

Postscript

As we approach the Millenium, a decade of physical change has altered the townscape, familiar shops are no more, and the constant quest for information about the past has itself changed our perception about that past.

No longer can we happily ascribe the town plan to Abbot Baldwin, but rather to Anselm, and it is no longer certain that St Mary's Square was the pre-Conquest market place. It appears more and more likely that the town developed gradually, rather than emerging in its present form in a matter of years.

There have been more archaeological finds, reviewed annually in the Proceedings of the Suffolk Institute of Archaeology and History. The site of St Saviour's Hospital was excavated prior to the building of the Tesco superstore, and elsewhere more evidence of Anglo-Saxon Bury has emerged.

The British Archaeological Association held their 1994 conference on Medieval Art and Architecture at Bury; when they publish their Proceedings, what we know of Bury's past will be yet more increased.

Since 1988 the A45 has become the A14, and there is once more a 'bus station. Partial pedestrianisation has been introduced to several streets, while a case could be made for more controlled crossings — especially now that sensors protect people in the latest versions. The cattle market has survived where it was, while modern retailing has brought Waitrose to the old Boby site, and Tesco where St Saviour's once stood.

Some of the old town centre shops — most recently Thomas Ridley's venerable grocery — have gone; when such premises reopen, they rarely perpetuate the same kind of business. The Suffolk Hotel was due to close at the end of 1996, and Debenham's in early '97. Yet not all is loss; some town centre properties once employed in commerce have reverted to residential use.

The conservation of the Unitarian Meeting House and the Nottyngham Porch of St Mary's Church, both badly needed eight years ago, has been accomplished. Recent cleaning and conservation of the stonework on the Corn Exchange has revealed details which have been virtually invisible for years.

The Cathedral now has its north extension, which provides much-needed vestries; facilities for meetings and conference opened in 1990. A second application to the Millenium Commission has been made for funds to build a central tower. The present stump, with its yellow bricks and metal spikes, is unsightly and should be replaced with something more appropriate and aesthetically pleasing — without delay.

Work has been completed on St Mary's Church tower, yielding much-needed space for parish use and Christchurch, Moreton Hall, has been opened.

Reflecting the past, the Manor House opened as a Museum in 1993. The following year, Samson's Tower, at the southern end of the Abbey Church's west front, opened as a Visitor Centre for the Abbey site. These have been created to the detriment of Moyses Hall, which served the town well as a Museum for almost a century. However, the Suffolk Regimental Museum may well find its home in a building nearby.

Set right in the heart of the historic town centre, Moyses Hall could well be developed as a truly local museum, reflecting the history of a proud and ancient town, and the life and work of those who lived and worked there.

The next decade will bring yet more of our past to light; perhaps it will also bring the means to conserve and improve more, to record and display more, to build better and to maintain Bury St Edmunds as a pleasant place in which to work and live in the next millenium.

Appendix : Population

Domesday Book states that 342 houses had been built on land which had been under the plough before the Conquest and so, as the valuation of the town had doubled between 1066 and 1089, we ought probably to envisage a community of about 680 families living in the town at that time.

When the chantries were dissolved in the reign of Edward VI, it was stated that there were more than 3,000 howseling people, ie communicants, as well as many children. A total population of about 4,500 is likely then.

The copy of the charter petition which has survived among the Yates MSS says that Bury St Edmunds was the most populous dry-walled town in England. The eighteenth and early nineteenth century guide books say that the charter petition revealed that there were 4,000 communicants in the time of Elizabeth I. Allowing for the high number of children in comparison with the total population, something in the region of 6,000 is indicated. Work on the parish registers and the figures given in the 1637 Church Brief also suggest a figure of 6,000 plus. The names of 608 able-bodied men over 16 years of age are recorded in the 1635 muster roll.

In connection with the tax for prosecuting the war against France, lists of inhabitants must have been made in many, if not all, parishes in 1695. The census of St James's parish in that year has survived, and lists 3,167 names, so about 6,000 plus is indicated for the total population.

When there was a small pox epidemic in 1757, a register was made of all the inhabitants of St Mary's parish, from which it can be seen that there were then 3,233 inhabitants in that parish. The population of the whole town must have been nearly double the number given for St Mary's parish. On the previous page from these totals, there is a note that, in 1733, there were 6,687 people, presumably in both parishes, of whom 2,625 had smallpox, 287 died and 642 were to have it.

From 1801 there are reliable figures available from the decennial censuses, which have been taken in each decade apart from the 1940s, when the 1941 census was omitted because of World War II. The figures for Bury St Edmunds are as follows:

Date	St James	St Mary's	Total
1801	3,565	4,090	7,655
1811	3,780	4,206	7,986
1821	4,769	5,230	9,999
1831	5,942	5,494	11,436
1841	6,269	6,269	12,538
1851	6,668	7,232	13,900
1861	6,714	6,604	13,318
1871	7,885	7,043	14,928
1881	9,441	6,670	16,111
1891	9,968	6,662	16,630
1901	9,979	6,276	16,255
1911			16,785
1921			15,937
1931			16,922
1951			20,056
1961			21,179
1971			25,661
1981			28,887
1991			32,562

Original Sources

A vast amount of original material for the history of Bury St Edmunds is available, both locally and in national collections, while Suffolk antiquaries of the past have often copied into their collections documents of which the original can no longer be found.

The records of the Borough of Bury St Edmunds and of the Guildhall Feoffment Trust have been used extensively; no history of Bury St Edmunds could be attempted without them. The wills proved in the Court of the Sacrist of St Edmunds and his successors are also of inestimable value. Archives of many organisations and families deposited in the Suffolk Record Office at Bury St Edmunds have also been used, and I hope that adequate clues to sources have been given in the text, for full references would not have been appropriate in a volume of this sort. A great debt of gratitude is due to all those who have edited and made available records elsewhere; it is hoped that in future there will be opportunities to discover the treasures of collections outside Bury St Edmunds.

Most of the illustrations come from the collections of the St Edmundsbury Museum Service and the Suffolk Record Office, Bury St Edmunds branch.

Select Bibliography

The literature for Bury St Edmunds is extensive and readers are advised to consult A.V. Steward, *A Suffolk Bibliography*, (Suffolk Record Society, 1979) as a starting point for further reading. More recent publications are noted in the *Newsletter* of the Suffolk Local History Council.

Battely, John, *Antiquitates S. Edmundi Burgi ad annum MCCLXXII perductae* (Oxford 1745)

Brakelond, Jocelin of, *Chronicle Jocelin of Brakelond*, ed by H.E. Butler, 1949

Davis, R.H.C., *The Kalendar of Abbot Samson of Bury St Edmunds and related documents* (1954)

Douglas, D.C., *Feudal Documents from the Abbey of St Edmunds at Bury* (Oxford, 1932)

Dymond, David and Martin, Edward (eds), *An Historical Atlas of Suffolk* (Ipswich, 1988)

Dymond, David and Northeast, Peter, *A History of Suffolk* (Chichester 1985)

Elliott, R.W., *The Story of King Edward VI School, Bury St Edmunds* (Bury St Edmunds 1963)

Fiske, Jane (ed), *The Oakes Diaries; Business, Politics and the Family in Bury St Edmunds, 1778-1827* 2 Vols (Woodbridge, Suffolk Record Society XXXII and XXXIII, 1990 and 1991)

Gillingwater, Edmund, *An Historical and Descriptive Account of Bury St Edmunds* (Saint Edmundsbury 1804)

Goodwin, A, *The Abbey of St Edmundsbury* (Oxford 1931)

Gransden, Antonia, 'The Alleged Incorruption of the Body of St Edmund, King and Martyr', *The Antiquaries Journal* LXXIV (1994)

Gransden, Antonia (ed), *Medieval Art and Archaeology at Bury St Edmunds* (BAA Conference Proceedings, forthcoming). Includes Statham, Margaret, 'The Medieval town of Bury St Edmunds' which modifies views given in this book.

Gransden, A., ed *Chronicle of Bury St Edmunds, 1212-1301* (1964)

'Baldwin, Abbot of Bury St Edmunds', *Proceedings of the Battle Conference on Anglo-Norman Studies*, IV, 1981

Harvey, John, *English Mediaeval Architects: A Biographical Dictionary down to 1550* (1954)

Hervey, Lord Francis, (ed) *Suffolk in the XVIIth Century: The Breviary of Suffolk by Robert Reyce, 1618* (1902)

The Pinchbeck Register (2 Vols, privately printed, 1925)

Corolla Sancti Eadmundi (1907)

H(ervey) S.A.H. (ed.) *Biographical List of Boys Educated at King Edward VI Free Grammar School, Bury St Edmunds, From 1550 to 1900* (Bury St Edmunds 1908)

James, M.R. *On the Abbey of St Edmund at Bury* (1895)

Lobel, M.D., *The Borough of Bury St Edmund's: A study in the Government and Development of a Monastic Town* (Oxford 1935)

MacCullough, Diarmaid, *Suffolk and the tudors: Politics and religion in an English County 1500-1600* (Oxford, 1986)

McCutcheon, Elsie, *Historic Bury St Edmunds* (Bury St Edmunds 1987)

Moore, Ellen Wedemeyer, *The Fairs of Medieval England, An Introductory Study*, (Pontifical Institute of Medieval Studies and Texts, LXXII, Toronto, 1985)

Pevsner, N., *The Buildings of England: Suffolk* (1974)

Powell, Edgar, *The Rising in East Anglia in 1381* (Cambridge 1896)

Proceedings of the Suffolk Institute of Archaeology (1848-date), *passim*, especially,

Blunt, C.E., 'The St Edmund Memorial Coinage' XXXI, 234

Gilyard-Beer, R, 'The Eastern Arm of the Abbey Church at Bury St Edmunds, XXXI, 256

M.D. Lobel, 'Detailed account of the 1327 rising at Bury St Edmunds,' XXI, 1931/3, 215-31

L.J. Redstone, 'The Liberty of Bury St Edmunds' XV, 1913/15, 200-11.

'"First Ministers Account" of the possessions of the Abbey of St Edmund,' XIII (1907/1909)

V.B. Redstone, 'St Edmunds Bury and town rental for 1205' XIII, 191-222.

S.E. West. 'Excavation of the town defences at Tayfen Road, Bury St Edmunds, 1968.' XXXII, 1970/72, 17-24

Dorothy Whitelock, 'Fact and Fiction in the Legend of St. Edmund' XXXI, 217

St Edmundsbury and Ipswich Parochial Libraries Committee, *Suffolk Parochial Libraries: A Catalogue* (1977)

Scarfe Norman, *Suffolk in the Middle Ages* (Woodbridge 1986)

Scarfe, Norman, *The Suffolk Landscape* (Bury St Edmunds, 1987)

Scarfe, Norman (ed and trans), Francois de La Rochefoucauld, *A Frenchman's Year in Suffolk, 1784* (Woodbridge, Suffolk Record Society, XXX, 1988).

Statham, Margaret, *Yesterday's Town: Bury St Edmunds* (Baron Birch, Whittlebury, 1992).

Tymms, Samuel, with additions by J.R. Thompson, *A Handbook of Bury St Edmunds* (1891) and other editions.

(ed), *Wills and Inventories from the Registers of the Commissary of Bury St Edmunds and the Archdeacon of Sudbury* (Camden Society 1850)

Historie of the Church of St Marie Bury St Edmunds (Bury St Edmunds 1854)

Whittingham, A.B.,'Bury St Edmunds Abbey: the Plan, Design and Development of the Church and Monastic Buildings'*Archaeological Journal*, CVIII (1951)

Wilson, Richard, *Greene King, A business and family history* (1983)

Yates Richard, *An Illustration of the Monastic History and Antiquities of the Town and Abbey of St Edmund's Bury* (1805)

Index

figures in italics refer to illustrations

Abbey
  Gate 12,*17*,26,
    27,*33*,56,105
  Abbot's Bridge
    . . . . 11,*16,35*,
    36
  Palace 28,*37*,106
  brazen doors 28
  buildings *34,35*
  Cellarer of . . . 13,25,27,
    55
  Chapel of the Charnel
    . . . . 27,28,*35*,
    36
  Chapter House . . . 31,40
  dissolution of . . 28,43,45,
    81,90,117
  dormitory 40
  episcopal exemption of
    27,43
  First Ministers' Accounts
    43,45,
    103
  fish ponds (Crankles)
   30
  Gesta Sacristarum 13
  grammar school . . 27,28
  master of 117
  guest house 43
  keeper of the Shrine of St
    Edmund 105
  King's Hall 40
  master mason of 44
  mill 40
  monks 27
  Norman Tower
    . . . . 26,27,*31*,
    32,33,34,35,38,
    67,*99*,106,*113*,119
  precinct of 11,12,13,
    26,27,28,*30*
  Sacrist of 43,55,56,
    89,90,105,117
  St John at the Hill, chapel
    of 27
  Well, chapel of 27
  Samson's Tower 28,*35*,44
  song school of . . . 27,117
  tower 28
  transept 40
  vineyard 27
  west front 27,28,*30*,
    34,35
  yard 104
Abbey Precincts 11,*38*
Abbo (of Fleury) 25,26
Abbot
  Anselm 12,13,26
    43,44,56,68,117

Baldwin 12,26,27
  44,55,91,117
Curteys 13
Edmund of Walpole . . *31*
Henry of Rushbrook . . *31*
Hugh I 28,90
John of Barnham 56
Ording *31*
Reve, John *96*
Richard of the Isle (of
  Ely) *31*
Robert II 43
Samson 13,27,28
  55,*71*,117
Abbots, skeletons of *31*
Adam, Robert . . . 89,*94*,104
Agnes, widow of William,
  son of Bartholomew
  .103
agricultural implements,
  manufacture of 91
Airey, Sir John 120
alderman 56,57,58,
  59,66,67,68,90,103,105
Alfred the Great, King . . 25
Almoner's Barns . . . 57,130
almshouses *16,54*,65
  71
Alwyne House *37*
Archaeological Institute
  .120
Arnold, John 13
assizes 56,80,105
Associated British Maltsters
 91
Athenaeum 13,105,
  120,*139*
Babwell, Friars of . . . 55,80
Bacon, Sir Nicholas, Lord
  Keeper of the Great Seal
 60
Badby, Thomas
  28,80,106
Bailiffs 90
Baker, Miss Mavis 25
bakers 90
banker 28,91
banleuca 11,26
Baret, John 13,44,*48*,
  89
Barnack, Northants 13
Batteley, John 118
Battely's *Antiquitates* 33
Baxter, James 45
Bede, the Venerable 25
Bedricesworth 11,26,55
Beeton's Lodge *138*
Bennet, Philip 70

Bereve, Joan 65
  Thomas 45,56,65,
    66,*79*
Bevan family 91
Black Death 68
Blomfield, Charles 119
Blomfield, Bishop (Charles
  James) Leedes, Edward
  . . . . 118,*125*
Bloomfield, A.W. 118
bookseller *96,98*
Botanic Garden . . *20,33,116*
Boyce, Dr, composer . . .105
Brabant 56
Bradfield Combust 82
St Clare 25
brewing 91,*96*
Bridge
  Abbot's 11,*16,35*,
    36
  Eastgate *63*
  Rothe 55
  St Botolph's, Raingate
    Street *63*
Bright, Thomas the elder
  d1587 57,67
  younger d1626 57,*60*,105
Bristol, Earl/Marquess of
  22,81
British Sugar Corporation
 91
Brome, Lord Charles, Lord
  Cornwallis 82
Browne, Adam of Brandon
 89
  Robert 105
Bryant, Count, Master of
  Ceremonies *113*
Buck, S. and N., engravers
  . . . . *41*
Buck, William 91
Bull, Thomas 69
Bunbury, H.W. *113*
Burgesses 45,57,58,
  67,68,90,103
Burrough, Sir James . . .118
Bury and Ipswich Railway
  . . . . *23*
  Bible 28
  Fair 13,*21,126*
  work . . . . 89 et seq
Bury and Norwich Post
  81,91,105
  118
  Free Press 81,119,
    129
  Post 81,*86*
  St Edmund's Psalter . . .*37*
butcher *100*

Butler, Philip 46
Butts Corner 106
Byfield, George *85*
carrier 14
Case, Philip James 81
Catteshall, Great Barton
 80
Cecil, Sir Robert 57
chaplains, parochial 43
Charles II, King 58
Charters 56,57,58,
  61,104
Church Briefs *18*
Churches
  advowsons of 45
  Baptist
    Garland Street
    46,47,65
    Lower Baxter Street
      (Ebenezer) 46
    Westgate Street
      (Rehoboth) 47
  Cathedral Church of St
    James 26,*38*,43,
    44,45,*49,50,51*,65,67,105,
    106,*113*,117,118,129
    altar of St Thomas à
      Becket 45,65
    building of . . 44 et seq
    chancel, 1711 45
    chancel by Scott, 1865-
      1869 . . . . 45,*50*
    library of 45,118
    paving of 45
    quire, 1970 44,45
    seating of 45
    vice (spiral staircase) in
   45
    window in 45
  curates or ministers of
    .45
  Independent 46
  Lecturers or Preachers of
    .45
  Methodist
    St Mary's Square . .52
    Brentgovel Street . .52
  Presbyterian . . . 46,47,*51*
  Quakers 46
  repair of . . . . . . 45 et seq
  Roman Catholic 47
  St Denis' 12,44,117
    Edmunds Roman
      Catholic *53*,120
    James's parish church
      see Cathedral . . . .
    John's 46,*51*,81,
      83
    Mary's . . 12,13,26,27,

143

42,43,46,47,54,65, 80,82,106,*114*,117,119
   angel roof 44
   Baret chapel . 44,*48*
   building of 43
   cadaver monument
   44
   Nottyngham porch
   44
   Peter's 46,*53*
   Unitarian (Churchgate Street) 46,*52*
   Whiting Street United Reformed Church . . . 46
Churchyard 11,27,*102*, 106,119
Clarkson, Thomas *84*
Clerk, Simon 44
Clopton, Dr Poley . . 65,*139*
cloth maker 45,*89*
   making industry 89
clothier 89
clothiers' company 89
Cnut, king 26,117
Coke, Arundel . . . 80,*83,84*, 139
   Sir Edward 80
College of Jesus *75*
comey ash *97*
Compostella, shrine of St James at 44
constables 81
Corder, William 80
Corn Exchange . . . 89,*93,94*
Cornish & Lloyd Ltd . . . 91
Coroner 58
Corporation 13,14,28, 43,45,46,56,57,58,59 62,64,69,79,80,*83,84*, 89,90,91,104,105
Corpus Christi College, Cambridge 28,103
Cottingham, L.N. *38*
council, town or borough 59,89
County Club *131*
Court
   Leet 80,81
   of Pie Powder 80
   Record 80
Court of Guardians of the Poor 58
coverlet weaving 89
Craske, Mr 120
Creed, George 59,*62*
cricket 106,*114*
Crisp, Edward . . . 80,*84,139*
Cupola House 22,*93*, 104,*137*
D'Ewes, Sir Simonds . . 118
Danes 11,25,26
Danyell, William 80
darnick weaver 89
Davy, D(avid) E(lisha)
   106

Henry, engraver
   . . . . *18,32,33*, *49,73*
Day, of Worcester (architect) 47
Deck, John *99*
Dickens, (Charles) 120
Discipline, Mr Alderman (Thomas) 105
Dispensary 69
Domesday Book . . . 12,127
dressmaker 105
Drury, Elizabeth 44
   Sir Robert 45,57
Dupecis, Mr 106
dyer 79
Eagle, Francis King . *62*,81
East Anglian Daily Times . 88
East Anglian Regiment . 82
Eastern Counties Navigation and Transport Co Ltd . . . 22
Eastgate Barns 55,130
Eastland, John 105
Ecgric 25
Edmund, King 939-946
   11
   King of the East Angles *see* St Edmund
Edward VI, king . . . 45,117
   the Confessor 12
Elizabeth I, Queen 28
Elvin, Cornelius 46,47
Ely, Cambs 25,26
Ely, E 92
Eugenius III, Pope 55
Fair, St Matthews . 105,*110*
fairs 57
Felton, Elizabeth, Countess of Bristol 118,*126*
   John 91
Fennell homes 65
Fire Brigade 78,*82*
fire
   engine 80
   plate 80
   Station 80,128
   1608 . . . . 89,*92*,103
   1882 130
Fornham All Saints . . 11,14
   St Martin 14,*22*
freedom of the borough . . 91
Frenze, Sir John 68
Frink, Dame Elizabeth . . *30*
fullers 55,89
Gage, Fr John 47
   Sir Thomas Rookwood 47
Gall, Abraham 59
Goal 47,57,80,81, *85,93*
gardener 65
Gardiner, Stephen *60*
gas lighting 81
Gates, of the town
   Eastgate 13,*16*,56

Northgate *17*,56
Risbygate 13,*17*,56
Southgate 56,68
Westgate 56
Gedge, Peter *86*
Geoffrey the porter 90
George II 81
   V 82,106,120
Gibraltar Barracks 82
glover 65
Godfrey, Richard, engraver
   . . . . *31,40*, *42,71*
Grafton, 3rd Duke of
   . . . . 81,*84*
Greene, Benjamin . . . 91,*96*
   King & Son plc . . 91,127 129
Greenstead, Essex 26
Grene, John 105
Grigby, Joshua 91
grocer *97*
Grose, Francis, the artist
   35,36
Guest, Ralph 65
guilds
   bakers 90
   Candlemas guild (Purification of Our Lady) 56
   cordwainers 90
   craft 90
   Dussegild 117
   linen and woollen weavers 90
   merchant 56
Guildhall
   in Guildhall Street
   . . . . 28,56,*59*, 60,61,*62*,65,80,81,*88*, 104,117,*125*
   Feoffees . . . 14,28,46, 56,57,*60*,*64*,65,66,67, 68,69,79,80,89,103, 104,105,120
   of the Guild of St Thomas à Becket 117
Guinness, Col and Mrs
   . . . . *87,115,126*
Gurdon, Mr Recorder . . 23
Haberdon 119
hadgovel 55
Haegelisdun (Hellsdon) 25,26
hairdresser 105
Handel, George Fredric
   105,106
Hardy, W.K. *39*
Hare, Mrs 65
Harrison, George 46
Harvey, John 105
Henhowe Heath 80
Henry VI *48*
Herbert de Losinga, Bishop of Norwich 27
Herfast, Bishop of Norwich
   27

Hermann, Archdeacon . . 25
Hervey, Admiral 81
   John, Lord 81
   1st Earl of Bristol . . . 105
Higham, T., engraver . . . *47*
highway surveyor 79
Hill, Professor Christopher
   58
Hitcham wood 57
Hodgson, Rt Revd Henry Bernard *51*
Hodson, Nathaniel
   . . . . 20,*33*,106
homage, payment to abbot in lieu of 56
Hooper, John Ridley *62*
Horning, Norfolk, St Benet's Hume in 26
Horringer Mill *101*
Hospital
   Clopton's 65,*75,139*
   Newmarket General Hospital 116
   St Audrey's, Melton
   116
   Mary's Day 66
   Nicholas 70,71
   Peter's 11,68,69 70
   Petronella's . . 68,*70,71*
   Saviour's 71
   Suffolk General
   . . . . 69,*76,77*
   West Suffolk General
   129
house of correction . . 66,68
Hoxne 26
Hubberty, Stephen 46
Hugo the taverner 103
Hugo, Master 28
Hustings, 1865 . . . . *86*
Inns and Hotels
   Angel 69,81,*87*, *102*,103,104,*139*
   Bushel 13
   Castle 103
   Cupola House
   . . . . 22,*93*,104,*137*
   Dog and Partridge . . *102*
   Fox 16
   Grapes Hotel 17
   Griffin *136*
   Half Moon 104,*108*
   King's Head *133*
   Magpie *83*
   Mermaid *102*
   One Bull 104
   Rising Sun *107*
   Six Bells *18*,28
   Suffolk Hotel . 14,*24*,103, *107*,108
Ipswich and Bury St Edmunds Railway
   15
ironmonger 91

Ixworth, Prior of 55
James I, King 57,58,*62*
Jarman, Oswald .. 105,*134*
Jermyn, Sir Edmund ...66
   Robert 57
Jocelin of Brakelond
   13,28,55
Johnson, Isaac, artist ... *70*
Justices of the Peace 58
Kembold, Peter 67
Kendall, J., engraver
   ....*35,36,98,*
        102,103,*139*
Kenyon, John 66
King's Lynn 14,67
King, Fred 91
   John 34
Kirby, Joshua, engraver . *49*
landmol 55
Lankester, Arthur *39*
Lark Navigation 22
Lark, River 11,14,27,
        38,55
Lathbury, artist *49*
Laud, Archbishop 46
lawyers 91
Leedes, Edward 118
Le Keux, Henry *48*
Liber Eliensis 25
library
   Bury and West Suffolk
   .... *125*
   Free (public) 80,128
   Grammar School 118
   St James's Church
   45,118
linen weavers 90
Linnet, River 11,*38*
Liszt 104
Lichfield, a surgeon 69
Lloyds bank 91,*99*
Lydgate, John, *Life of St*
   Edmund 103
Mackenzie, artist *48*
Macro, Cox 104
   Thomas *22*,*93*
Magna Carta 27,104,
        112
Mallowes, John 91
malting 67
Maps
   Downing (1740) *16*
   Lenny (1823) .. 14,*20*,119
   Warren (1747) .. 106,*113*
market 57
   butter *88*
   cattle 89,*93*,127
        128
   corn 89
   pig 127
   place 11,43,55,
        90
   provision 89,127
   tolls 89,127
Market Cross 14,*23*,46,
   57,67,89,*92*,94,104,128

Masonic Lodge *18*,28
Mayor 59
McAdam, James 58,79
Members of Parliament
   81
millers 67
minstrels 105
Miro Press 47
Moody, Samuel 46
Morrell, Wilberforce ... 106
Moyses Hall 12,13,14,
   18,*32*,*50*,66,*72*,*73*,81
Municipal Corporations
   Act, 1835 .... 58,*62*
Museum of East Anglian
   Life 91
music 105
Musical Festival *114*
mystery plays, N-Town
   cycle 103,104
Nair, Mr 106
Non-conformists .. 46,58
Nottyngham, John .. 44,*48*
Nowton Court 42,128
Oakes, James 28,*62*,91
        99
Observer Corps *88*
Odeham, Margaret 56
Oliver, Basil *134*
organist 65
Orridge, John 80,*85*
Ouse, Little 11
Overseers of the Poor ...67
Oxford, Earl of ... 105,106
Pack, Major Richardson
   .... *37*
Pageant,
   1907 .... *112*
   1959 .... *112*
   mediaeval 104
   St Edmund 104
Paine, Clive 44
parish officers 79
Passerini, Signora 106
Payne, Humphrey 46
peruke maker 65
pest houses 69
pillory 57
plague 68,69,*72*
Police Station 81,128
Poor Law Amendment Act,
   1834 66
Portmanmoot (borough
   court) 55
portrait painter 105
Post Office *99*,*132*
printer *98*
Probate Registry 28,*35*
Provost's House 65
Pynner, Francis *75*,103
Quarter Sessions
   58,80,105
Quinton, George, artist
   .... *38*,*116*
Rackham, John *96*
Radford, Dr Ralegh 44

Railway Station
   Eastgate *24*,106
   Northgate 15,*23*
Randall, James 13
Recorder 57,58,59,
        91
Redgrave, architect ...103
Rednall, William, architect
        35
Redstone, Lilian Jane ... *64*
Remond, Herman 13
Rep silver 55
Reynolds, Sir Joshua ...81
Richardson, Sir Thomas 91
Ridley, Thomas *92*
Risbygate Cross 11
Robert Boby & Son 91
Robinson, Henry Crabb
   46
Roger the Porter 90
Rookes, Letitia *113*
Rougham 25,26,*70*
Royal Archaeological
   Institute 106
   Show, 1867 106
Sancroft, (William)
   Archbishop of
   Canterbury 118
Sankey, Dr (Charles) ..106
schools
   Anglican 120
   charity 119,*122*
   Charles Blomfield's in
      Lower Baxter Street 119
   County Grammar,
      Northgate Street ...120
   Grammar School
   57,68,69,
      80,104,106,119,120,
      122
   boys of 119
   governors 119
   in Eastgate Street
   117,118,
      121
   in Northgate Street
   .... 118,*121*
   on the Vinefield
   .... *122*,128
   Guildhall Feoffment
      Boys' *123*
   Commercial .. 120,*124*
   King Edward VI
   117,128
   Lancastrian, College
      Street 119
   Mr Crew's, Lower Baxter
      Street 119
   Eastland's, Angel Hill
  119
   Wood's, at the College
  119
   St Edmundsbury
   .... 120,*124*
   James's Middle
   118,120
      128

National 119,*124*
Silver Jubilee, Grove
   Road 120,128
Scott, Mrs (formerly Miss
   Young) 106
   Sir Gilbert 45,*50*
scrivener 67
Sexton's Meadow
   .... 68,69,*72*
shearmen 89
Shire Hall 27,28,80,
      83,104,117
shops
   Andrews & Plumpton
   12
   Burton's *132*
   Dudley's 46
   Fenton's *135*
   Gibbs pie shop *100*
   Groom's *98*,*135*
   Hunter and Oliver .. *132*
   Jarman's *135*
   Martin's (formerly
      Boot's) *132*
   Mothercare *133*
   Old Curiosity Shop ... *98*
   Palmer's 12
   Ridley's *96*,*97*
   Quant's *92*
   Spanton's *135*
Shudy Camps, Cambs .. 19
Sigeberht 11,25,26
      43
smallpox 69,*72*,76
Smyth, Anne 54
   John (commonly called
      Jankyn) 44,54,56,
      59,*62*
Spanton, William 81
Spink, John 28
spinning 89
St Edmund 4,11,25,
   26,27,28,*29*,*30*,47,104
   Brewery 91
   Liberty of 27,*30*,66
   Edmund's Hill 26
   Working Man's
      Association
   66
   Peter's pit 69
St Edmunsbury Post 81
Start-rite shoes 92
steam roller, Aveling Porter
      78
street cleaning 81
   lighting 79
   names, 15th century
   15
Streets and Roads
   Abbeygate Street
   12,14,43,
      44,46,*48*,92,98,99,129,
      135,*136*,*137*
   Albert Street 14
   Angel Hill 13,14,46,
      76,79,80,82,*102*,103,
      104,119,128,*134*

Lane 69,92	Mildenhall Road .. 14,*22*, 127,*135*	Victoria Street 14	Torksey, Lincs 66
Athenaeum Lane *18*		Westgate Street	Tourist Information Centre
Barton Road 70	Mustow Street ... 26,*133*, 134	.... 11,47,71, 96,*100*,104,129,*134*	 80,128
Brentgovel Street 52			Town Clerk 57,58,89, 91
Bridewell Lane .. 13,66, 125	Northgate Street *10*,11,12, 14,*24*	Whiting Street ... 46,66, 138	Tymms, Samuel 106
Burmans Lane 65,79		Sudbury 14,15,43, 81,118	*Valor Ecclesiasticus* 25
Butter Market ... 14,91, 100,*108*,114	Orchard Street 14	Suffolk Regiment 81,82	Vickers Group 91
	Out Risbygate 11,68,69, 70,82	Tithe Payers Association. 46	Vinefield 106
Chalk Road 68			waites 105
Chequer Square *18*,76,89	Westgate 106	Yeomanry Cavalry 82,*87*	Walker, Richard 66
Churchgate Street	Paddock Pool 13		Warren, Thomas *42*
.... 12,13,46, *51*,66,68	Parkway 106	sugar beet factory .. 91,127	Wastell, John 44,*49*
	Prospect Row 14	surgeon 77	water supply 81
College Street 66,*75*, 119	Pump Lane 65	Surgeon 69	weaving 89,90
	Punch Lane 13	Sutton 25	Wesley, John 46
Cordwainers Street ... 90	Raingate Street .. *63*,117, 128	Swegn Forkbeard, King of England and Denmark	West, Dr S.E. 12,25,*64*
Cornhill 14,80,89, 98,*128,132*			West Suffolk College 11,128
	Risbygate Street 68,104, *107,124*,127	 26	County Council ... 27,*30*
Crown Street .. 13,14,27 *96*		Symonds, Professor (John) 26	Review Order . *10*,11,14, 127
	Rotten Row 14,89	tailor 65	Westley 14
Cullum Road 106	St Andrews Street 13,65,89, 91,127,128,*134*	Tassell, William 103	Whittock, engraver *33*
Eastgate Street 13,14,15, 23,66,106,*120*,134		Tate and Lyle 91	Wilkins, William 85
	Botolph's Lane 47	Telemann (George Philipp) 106	William, King, the Conqueror 12,26
Field Lane 14	Edmund's Place ... 14		windpump *83*
Garland Street 79	Johns Street .,13,14,*24*, 46,87,*133*	Teyfen 55	Winthrop, Forth 118
Guildhall Street ... 13,*18*, *100*,120		Thackeray, (W.M.) ... 120	John, Governor of Connecticut 118
	Mary's Square 11,43,65	*The Bury Post* 81,*86*	
Hatter Street *126*		*Morning Chronicle* 86	Governor of Massachusetts 118
High Street *10*,12	Schoolhall Street 66,117	*Suffolk Mercury* .. 81,104, 119	
Hollow Road 70,91			workhouse 66,68,*74*, *75*,119
Honey Hill 80,117, 118	Sicklesmere Road . 80,*85*	Theatre Royal *109,110*, 129	
	Southgate Street .. 47,*64*, 71,106		Wright family 97
King's Road 14,119		Thetford 14	Robert, Lord Chief Justice 118
Looms Lane 14,119	Southgate Green 71	Thingoe Deanery 43	
Lower Baxter Street 119	Sparhawk Street *10*,11,*24*, 80	Union Workhouse 66,*75*	Young Men's Institute 120
			Young, Arthur 82
Master Andrews Street 66	Traverse, the 14,104	Thompson, George *130*	Zeppelin Raid *88*
		toll collector 89	

Addendum, 1996

Delete Little Ouse 11; Miro Press 47; Guildhall 81;

Amend Bloomfield, A.W. to Blomfield, Sir Arthur; Airey, Sir John to Airy, George

Add under Abbey, Samson's Tower 140;

under Abbot: Anselm 140 and Baldwin 140;

under Churches - Cathedral, extension 140; Christchurch, Moreton Hall 140; Nottyngham Porch, St Mary's 140; Unitarian 140;

Corn Exchange 140; Ely, Cambs 11; Great Ouse 11; Hellesdon 25,26;

under Inns & Hotels, Suffolk Hotel 140; Manor House 81,140; Moyses Hall 140; Ridley, Thomas 140;

Royal Bank of Scotland 12; St Benet's Hulme 26;

under Streets & Roads: Buttermarket 89; Honey Hill *131;* St Mary's Square 140;

St Saviour's Hospital 140; Suffolk Regimental Museum 140

ENDPAPERS: First edition of Warren's plan of the town, 1747. The ditch along the west side of the precinct wall had been filled in; it shows the town gates, old course of the River Linnet, and a concentration of building within the mediaeval town centre and its suburbs.